Freedom on Both Ends of the Leash

Written by
Ara Gureghian and Spirit

For information about this title or to order other books and/or electronic media, contact the publisher:
SixLegged Productions
853 Vanderbilt Beach Rd #245
Naples, FL 34108
www.theoasisofmysoul.com

ISBN:
978-0-9960837-0-6 Print
978-0-9960837-1-3 eBook

Photo Gallery: http://beemerchef.smugmug.com/
Cover and Interior design by: 1106 Design
Cover Photo: Ara Gureghian

Dedicated to

My three Best Friends.

My Dear Mother who stood by me so filled with love for 65 years.

My Dear and only Child Lance who passed on too early, yet gifting us with his 26 years of pure Living.

My sweet Pit and buddy Spirit who patiently sat by me while writing these pages, as I heard him say one day "Everyone has a dog, can we also get one so I will have someone to play with while you are writing?"

Thank You.

S O MANY TO SAY "Thank You" to. So many, it would fill a book on its own. Throughout these seven years, the beginnings were the two of us. Spirit and I. Within such a short time a community was born. And what a community! You all know who you are. "Thank You" for your support, your friendships, your hospitality, your generosity, your kind words and quite often clearing those murky windows surrounding us letting the light in.

I can never thank enough my good friend Dee, who day in and day out corrected my grammar and allowed these pages to express what I meant.

First of all...

I T IS ABOUT 100 DEGREES. The solar fan is only blowing hot air, and now, back in the middle of this desert, the wet soaking and dripping bandana around my neck is giving me a resemblance of coolness. I feel as it is a go. I can write. I see the pages and I need to start over. They have been amazingly dormant for too long to be again picked up and placed on this empty slate. The road we have been on has brought us back here at The Oasis, these few acres in Big Bend Flats, Texas. For more reasons than one, I am ready to put it all down on paper. I hope I can do it. A personal challenge which will take me through the steps that have led us here, seven years later, two wanderers and a freedom sought dictating their whereabouts.

About us

THERE REALLY IS NO BEGINNING as there will be no end. It is all imagination. A human made concept to make us believe so. This book has no chapters, a continuous life story. Chapters are only moments put together back to back creating these illusions we have been so programmed with. The reality of life is in the heart. Timeless. There is however within all of us, a first breath and a last one. I witnessed both with my son Lance. It has been ten years now, and what can I say, think, feel, shout and murmur that I have not already expressed. For three years after he left us, I went on with what is called the normal life. The stage turned foreign and I did not succeed. Some will get lost in alcohol, some within drugs and will sit in that corner, that one, the one with the wide screen television and the blank stare, waiting for their own time to come. Patient or impatient, they will remain immobile throughout the moments passing by, one click at a time of the big hand on the clock. It is not my character or Spirit's to do so. Feelings are part of my core, the trunk of my life. A little over seven years ago, I sold and gave away what little I had, rescued Spirit, Spirit rescued me. I attached a sidecar to my getting old motorcycle, a 1996 BMW R1100GS, collected some camping gear, and as simple as that, without ever turning back physically or mentally, we left. Don't assume wrong on the idea. There is a romance about being on the road.

It always has been there for me, but this time I could not call it romance. It was as twisting that throttle on a dark path into a somber tunnel with a broken headlight and brakes never holding. A time with no faith or hope and a multitude of questions. I only knew I trusted myself, that spark and those voices inside me. I felt I made the right decision even if wrong by all means of a logical life anyone else would want to live. It still is today as the roads have been our arteries into the depth of this beautiful and vast country, into my soul and mind as the graveled shoulders have been the meeting places with others sharing their own journey. It was important to write down my thoughts on pages which were my therapy and sounding boards. They still are. I bought a camera which led to many photos. I have always traveled. Traveling however is today another entity, separate and unlike living on the road. It is the term Lance and I would use when we went out with no plans, "hang out". Except this is life's "hanging out". A new challenge surfaced these past few months. It was my Mother's time to say "Good Bye" from a hospital bed in Munich, Germany. This book is now more than ever a need, a tool to rehabilitate myself one more time by writing my own past path and emerging as I have done before. My entries in our journal accumulated these past years. There are more than 800. It is time to insert and bind them. As Lance's last words were "It's all good".

Freedom on Both Ends of the Leash

THE FIRST DAY A BLUR, the same for the first week. November 2006? Very obscure. I do remember having a GPS, one of those antique ones with a screen as large as a postage stamp. I must have not been paying much attention, if any, as a few hours later the road became familiar. It took us right back to where we started. Was I in the best of spirits? I cannot remember that aspect either. I do remember the frustration, a knot in my stomach as "was this a sign while being back at mile marker one?" How difficult could it be to just go West? It became our first but not last time getting lost in a circle. Not very promising while trying to put some distance between us and Georgia, hoping to make it to Alabama on that first night. Of course we did not. Not that day. From the first night on I needed to put my thoughts into written words knowing writing would be part of my therapy. My laptop, as the GPS, by today's standards had been around for too many years, yet daily, my own conversations never stopped. The first few pages are lost somewhere in space, it picks up when we arrived in Texas not long after. Throughout my working days of past years, I always managed to take a few months vacation. Generally in summer times when my profession had been catering as a Personal Chef to my

1

wealthy clients in Naples, Florida. During the summers they went on their own vacations all over the country and the world. I always avoided Texas. Even winter in this State at that time being unthinkable. I will always remember the joke between us riders "get in and get out, if you can in one day". How little I knew! Stopping in San Antonio, while accepting a few nights of hospitality due to bad weather, changed and shaped the years to come. Had I ever heard of Big Bend? Of course not, as I still come across many Texans who themselves have no clue of its whereabouts. It is a must my friend said, as I looked at the map and saw this giant green blob which depicted a monster size park of almost a million acres and a couple more million west, east and north of it including a National and State Park. Across the Rio Grande was Mexico. Nothing wrong with that picture. Winter was not such a good time to head north, and further west could wait a bit longer. Alabama, Louisiana, Mississippi, the wheels had been turning for over 1,000 miles.

From San Antonio, our first stop was Sanderson, riding on smooth roads and Highway 90 empty of traffic. The only jam present, my mind debating strongly if I was trying to escape the pain with such an uncertain future, or would this truly be our therapy for the years to come? I realized very quickly Spirit was not going to have any difficulties absorbing the unknown which laid ahead filled with its contained mysteries. Here and there, in the sun, shade, on his pad or the ground, soft or hard, wherever we were, he made his home. New smells by the thousands? By the millions? Who knows. I found him content from the first mile on, a huge relief when feeling a bit apprehensive taking a chance with him having never heard his opinion. I remember being on numerous dog and pit bull forums announcing our future path. Most everyone thought pretty much it was a crazy and dangerous one. An insane idea to embark on such a journey against all odds. With a pit bull! Those were the comments. We sure have proven them wrong. Lance also boarded with us. As odd as it may sound, I felt him running and flying nearby. Not to stop us, but with a smile never holding back. It allowed me to often be pleased from early on and bring back, as a superimposed reel, fond memories, the doubt grabbing life by its horns slowly vanishing. I felt as though having not taken a single breath since we left Georgia. The horizons opened and I began feeling a blanket slowly lifting off me as on an ocean with no breeze, the welcome unmaintainable throughout those moments. Some rain mixed in with that sweet smell of wet dirt and the cotton balls in the skies playing hide and seek while looking ahead, I was also looking above. Sanderson appeared. A quaint small Texas town 160 miles from Big Bend, actually from Terlingua, our destination. Too late to push on, this would make our entrance, our grand finale in full daylight the next day so much more grandiose, while thinking in the meantime, what three million acres of mostly empty spaces would look like. First impressions. Right? A small campground on the left with a wooden pink pig mailbox, a space also doubled as an RV Park, the only game in town and a friendly owner. I forget, a nice shower much needed. My first taste of Texas BBQ down the road after setting up, and I was ready for my dreams and Spirit to keep me warm for the night. It did not quite happen that way. We were not told about the train. That train which seemed to be passing right through the tent more or less on the hour with a perfect resemblance of an earthquake. Earplugs slightly deadened the sound, but not the tremor. I woke up tired. The on-going commotion did not seem to have bothered Spirit. I could not recreate a peaceful night. I knew many of them would be right around the corner. Let's move on. Which we did.

We reached Alpine thinking we had arrived at our destination. It was only the beginning of a long road taking us further. Mountains in Texas? We climbed a mile when I noticed a road bearing to the right with its sign "Mile High Road". I wanted to stop every 100 feet and take a photo. I straightened up on the seat breathing deeper than ever as the air so clean. Spirit glancing right to left, left to right, nonstop as he seemed to not be able to contain himself. He must have known this would be an important destination. A hill came up as a funnel lined by man made short cliffs cut into the road. We stopped as my breath was taken away. To this day, that crest remains stunning when camping at The Oasis and coming back from a day in Alpine on the same Highway 118. The heart stopping view has never ceased to exist. It is sensory overload, an aspect of this journey which never fails, only increases as will my senses. We moved on and every few miles a 360 degree span offered new backgrounds and silhouettes against the skies which had turned a clear blue. The feelings were a long way off from any words anyone could express including myself. The wheels kept turning and a present anticipation wanted to meet a future now not so distant as all would remain within this lifetime's memory bank. Magical, spiritual, all while being beamed into a different medium, a stage unfelt and unseen before. There would be many such times throughout the coming years as I have now found out. Right then and there, we met the true Texas.

The last hill appeared while at first concealing and then exposing the little town of Terlingua. The one ridge which to this day I describe as coming up on the end of the world. Unless entering the park, one cannot travel any further south without crossing into Mexico. This was the end of the line. A single row of houses, a few restaurants, empty dwellings as abandoned carcasses, couple motels, all making this town about ten miles long. Nothing really stood out, yet deep inside I felt a change I was not even trying to figure out. We set up camp on flat ground next to a hill which belonged to an RV park. Free camping, or close to it with a back country permit, was only available in the park. We joined other riders and camped together. Each tent a different color forming our own small village and motorcycles parked, each of different purposes. Strictly off road, dual sport and some black top only. We took a few rides together mainly on one of the most beautiful roads in this country called River Road, joining Terlingua to Presidio. The conditions of being there went downhill the following days. I became ill and tried, while desperately letting time go by, to feel better with the hope of a change in course. Unfortunately, waiting did not do much good and I searched for a doctor.

We embraced the 170 miles round trip to Alpine. We did find a doctor who wrote me a prescription for a Z-Pack, a pharmacy and I survived through it. We lived through it so well that all of a sudden we were what I called "in the zone", that would be "the desert zone". A few days later, a local retired fireman and avid motorcyclist, Roger, whom we called Uncle for reasons still obscure to me to this day, allowed us to camp on his land some ways off the main road half way through Terlingua. We had power, water and showers nearby. Luxuries and the zone lasted a couple months. The calendar vanished further as if it never existed. My wrist untanned from wearing a watch in the past started to pick up my arm's color, time lost its meaning, its value, we jumped into the "now". Terlingua will do that to you. Obligatory siesta every day, when the already quiet town plunged into a total ghost town. The western side of the town is literally called the Ghost Town. This is where the cemetery lies as well as remains of dwellings which harbored the past cinnabar miners. The mineral from which the harmful mercury was produced. Christmas came, followed by New Year's Eve and New Year's Day having not moved. Spirit and I were in for a surprise one morning. One common for the northerners. Ice. A tropical setting for weeks, now all frozen including leaky sprinklers designing their own beautiful ice art off the ground and for the first time Spirit found his water bowl frozen. We played a short game of Frisbee as he ended up eating the pieces of ice scattered on the now frozen ground. Our riding companions left one at a time as the array of tent colors dwindled away when we visited them. The first of many friends we would meet and unfortunately never see again. Such is the road. There is no schedule, only coincidences of meetings. It is a fact which took me a while to understand as us without a timetable, everyone else had one.

The rides went on as did the cooking. Being a picky and healthy eater, my meals remained inexpensive from their basic non-refrigerated ingredients. Down through the park we went. Old Maverick Road, the outlook to Boquillas, The Basin, Sotol Look Out, back on River Road and this time on to Marfa for some great pizza at the Pizza Foundation, a Falafel sandwich at the Food Shark, endless destinations. More roads. Fort Davis, the Observatory, the pools of Balmorhea, Marathon and its papercrete homes. Another wave of riders showed up. Some with trailers harboring their motorcycles, bunk bed and full kitchen, their company a change for us. The days kept my mind occupied, yet slowly "moving on" filtered in. Many had traveled further west and the conversations regarding those spaces tantalizing, intriguing and appealing. I had no doubt we would come back, as already seeing this space for a winter home base, knowing too well it would take more than a lifetime to explore its acres. And we left. A day mixed with many emotions, a bit torn about going or not. A few miles away my impairment left me as my heart filled with emotions of new roads and experiences awaiting. For the first time, I felt addicted to the lifestyle, as I started thinking about my own roots, my Armenian ancestry filled with much history and a gypsy blood. I had many times been to Egypt where my grandparents lived in Cairo and camped in the deserts with the Bedouins. Simple life while setting up their villages of all sizes, carrying on their camels their basic necessities and hunting for fresh meat. Such life always made a point with me, maybe an envy of their freedom to come and go and as us, a path only dictated by the weather. Old Faithful was my camel, Spirit my moral support and everything else a dog can give through their unconditional love.

El Paso. We rode some freeway from Van Horn on and rolled at our own pace not trying to keep up with the traffic, being fully loaded with camping gear. The three of us tipped the scale at 1,200 pounds! Passed El Paso, the Chiricahua Mountains were ahead. We took Highway 9 westbound right along the border. I spent a few months in those hills not long ago while securing a job as a cook at the Southwestern Research Station after Lance passed away, having let go of my business incapable anymore of handling it. The job did not last long being an angry man at the time clashing with everyone, including the other cook, a drunk with not much experience in a kitchen. I was gently let go and such a shame as she got fired a month later. Wilcox, Benson, Fort Bowie, Cochise Stronghold, Tombstone. All so familiar and glad to be back with certainly a better frame of mind. I felt a circle had closed in and yet, I could not or tried to figure out why and its meaning. There would be much time for such thinking. I knew with the weeks and months and eventually years going by, time would bring some clarity toward this present of ours. Maybe some answers. There was not much physical comfort in our daily life. On the other hand, not uncomfortable as all is a compromise, the comfort being mental. Someone wrote me *"I am at home in my own Soul"*, how true and still is. The Chiricahuas stood behind us within days satisfying my hunger for the miles westbound. We went with the present flow and a couple days later found ourselves in Anza Borrego. I looked around not quite comprehending where we were. I thought it would be a park in a desert, not a town. I did not look at maps very well. Who needs maps when there really is not a final destination. I understood while I turned the pages, Borrego Springs is indeed a town in the middle of Anza Borrego. It all made sense. We stopped by the Visitors Center to get my bearings in order. Living on the road versus traveling had not yet caught up with me, feeling in a bit of a daze, floating on clouds as maybe still on an outing going to a picnic. Much discovery at the Center including information on campgrounds where everyone could be and was, bumper to bumper, enjoying each other's walls in the form of their multicolored RVs. Backtracking a bit further east, I discovered one could camp free for as long as they wanted. In reality, 30 days but no one was checking. We headed out of town towards a giant Playa laid out as though waiting for our arrival. A few other campers here and there, far enough from each other to introduce ourselves but not quite in our line of vision. Barely dots on the horizon. True happiness discovering such welcoming open spaces. We settled, I cooked, Spirit ate and played. That was his job. There seemed to be more than enough room and impressed at our find. A great night's sleep and we woke up to clear blue skies and mild temperatures. "I'll take that"

I told myself. Not a great day for photography as I tried to avoid the harsh daylight, there would be many cloudy days ahead of us. I only relaxed the first days, the space inviting and met some of the campers from all walks of life on a Friday night. Bob had been living on the road for a few years under the radar, meaning no phone, address or bank account. With the coast not too far from Anza Borrego, in the midst of refurbishing a sailboat, he was close to his departure towards some islands in the Pacific. Solid gold was his currency. I didn't quite know what to say, but it sounded fascinating. John and Lisa were part timers, working a few months out of the year to create some income enabling them to live the other remaining times on the road. There were a few more. Some camped out for a week, a month, a few days. Friday nights were their pot-luck and bonfire get together while sharing stories and a few drinks. We attended as I sat back, more observing than anything else and distinguishing the many personalities present, most respectful with each other. At times, when politics made its presence on stage, some were not so considerate and left after standing up and pacing as if such behavior would make others change their opinions. I found it interesting, all so far from my own path. Humans I think, are so complex. Each so alike and yet so different.

We were there to ride as we saddled up the following day. I opened the map and the main first page showed having already come across coast to coast leaving me bewildered. Too fast? Maybe. Yet, it had been months. I was not able to reach into the depth of the spaces we had been experiencing. I needed to physically and mentally slow down. I could not keep running trying to stay ahead of what was churning deep inside me. Lance here, Lance there. Sometimes I did not feel his presence and it saddened me. He must have been spending time with his Mother. I called her as still very much in touch, and yes, he was with her. He would be back with those brightly lit green eyes and an aura which never quits. The rides. I saw Palm Canyon Drive but I wanted to tour Fonts Point to Fonts Wash for no apparent reason. Just because. Another road called its name louder, Rockhouse Canyon. That would be the one while experiencing the unpaved roads of Anza Borrego. They were of deep sand and rocky at times, all looking so innocent and Old Faithful's one wheel drive, even with knobby tires, got me in trouble. Reality hit me when spinning and moving sideways instead of a forward momentum I would have much more appreciated. A delicate usage of the clutch and the throttle only got me deeper. Soon, I could not even see the rim and only spokes were protruding out of the sand. I tried my shovel, my jack, a piece of carpet under the tire, all with no hope. A Duh! moment. Only noon, and even though a weekday, someone was bound to come by and rescue us. We had food, water, shade for Spirit. No excitement needed, as two or three miles away, I saw a resemblance of some vehicles we could walk to. Hopefully not a mirage. While still standing and trying, I heard an engine in the distance. Its grumble growing louder and there appeared this beautiful all decked out Jeep. Fully loaded, lifted, winch, tall jack, big shovel, you name it. The owner's name was Mike and he seemed more excited than myself to try out his new toy, which even from a few feet away smelled like a new car. It did take him three tries to turn us around as there was no sense to go any further in the direction planned. Back on the black top. It would be as such in the Anza Borrego area. Unfortunately, this being only a small taste of what most of the roads were like. I thought hard about the incident. I could not take such an aspect lightly and could not rely on what others would tell me about road conditions. A sidecar is not a 4 × 4 or a motorcycle on two wheels. It has its own challenges which few understood. I had to be more visual, stop and hike when in doubt. It is a habit which remains even today. We stayed on the paved roads the following days. Roads S3, 78, S2 southbound to Ocotillo, Granite Mountain and its valley, all criss crossed by the unpaved roads as arteries in the park's heart. Beautiful winding roads with a higher level of a peace of mind. Maybe some day in the distant future, in another life, we will come back with a Jeep and explore what we could not these days. Saturday came, the best day of the week as the Farmers Market took place in downtown Borrego Springs.

Fresh food! A busy shopping day. Fingerling and purple potatoes, my favorites, homegrown heirloom tomatoes, fresh greens, radishes soaked in water and lemon juice, avocados, more. Out of room, Spirit shared his seat with the purchased produce as we headed back to cook, enjoy and indulge.

Death Valley was calling. Perfect time of the year. Moving day arrived but I could not. It was January 26th, the third anniversary of Lance's passing away. The day did not crumble, Mother Nature held me up and so did my own Mother whom I was able to call. This is what I wrote in my journal that day for Lance's first anniversary.

"Three years ago today, January 26th of 2004 at 10 p.m., the life support umbilical cord which kept a human being alive was pulled. At 10:30 p.m., being granted another 30 minutes in this world of ours, a human being managing to say with his last breath 'It's all good', left us and departed for another dimension. He is my Son Lance, my only child, my buddy and my friend. My own world had crumbled a long time before that day. I will never forget receiving the phone call expressing a cancer tumor had been found in his liver. That was in 2002. Hope never leaves the mind, but when the prognostic of it being discovered was already in stage four, a wall instantly went up, a wall which deep down I knew we were never going to be able to get over. We searched for a cure as far as Europe, as far as experimental procedures, all with no avail. This is not about me, but about Lance. We are not supposed to see our children go away, at least that is what they say. It has added a layer to my life which is so dark and permanent around the clock that I live with it constantly day after day, hour after hour. I have tried to come to terms with it but it has left me numb as I have to accept it but do not understand. This journey at

times would have been in his company, but it is not. I try to fill his shoes because it is what he would have wanted me to do. To continue on living and experiencing the beauty and experiences which being on the road offers, and most of all, to share with you all as he would have liked to. Lance was a copy of me. Improved however. He was a kind man always thinking about others, his Mother and Father, his family, his friends, everyone around him. His popularity amazed me. Sometimes I would have to wait patiently for some quality time with him. They all came to see Lance, to talk to him, laugh with him with an always obvious bond. I cannot help smiling when I think about his beautiful girl friends. When witnessing his relationships, I could always tell their own passion toward him. 'Well done Son' I would tell him. He was born with a natural aura. I continuously thought about it as a permanent halo. He had this magnetism within him which drew people towards his presence. Including me! I would get so much of a kick, for lack of better words, just watching his interactions with his surroundings. He was after all my Son, part of me lived in him and we had so many similarities. Same handwriting, same gestures, same clothing and shoe size and a great outlook on life. He loved 'nice'. He loved Nike, Armani, Mountain Hardware and Ducatis. He loved good food. Not just good food but excellent food, refined food. He knew about all the great restaurants, all the places to go out and eat according to what anyone felt in the mood for. A pretty good cook himself, so many times we had talked about opening a restaurant together, maybe called 'Father and Son'. It never happened. He was so good with people he would have taken care of the front and me, the kitchen. He wanted a motorcycle in such desperate ways, a red Ducati Multistrada. We went to look at them more than once. We never bought one. So many ideas never realized when he was healthy. So many. Today I often live with the guilt of not having taken the steps for those realizations that he wished so much. It was always a bad time, the wrong time, school, money, time for this instead of that. He now continues living within me. I share this Journey with him as he watches over me every step of the way. I go on through these days of past, present and future, with the hope that this is what he would have seen, experienced, wrote and photographed. An Oasis is a source of life. My Oasis is Lance. My days are filled with his thoughts as time allows me to do so, unobstructed within this clear and open path that I have chosen. I go on because he said 'It's all good'. Remember? Hug your kids today, hug your family, hug your friends, hug a stranger. Don't put off your plans, make some if you do not have any. Don't put off until tomorrow what you could do today, the rest will wait, 'they' might not. Sometimes life cannot be fixed, everything else can. My day will go on today as every day, more special than the other ones, filled with more memories than ever, a quiet day as three years ago. I know that you will also have some kind thoughts having met today an incredible young man, my son Lance."

We were up early the next morning. A bad night with hardly any sleep. The images from three years ago replaying over and over. There seemed to be no escaping. I had to deal with it. We packed and were back on the road. The first of many times picking our next destination, but going the other way, slowly learning about total freedom. I surprised myself saying "Why not?" and finding it to be a very logical question. North, the Mojave Preserve, the high desert, it would be colder. That's what remained on my mind as we backtracked towards Salton Sea and on inadvertently the busy freeway, Highway 10. Never in my wildest dreams I thought we would be 100 miles from Los Angeles. The fumes, the traffic, the madness of a present urban jungle, as I will call it for years to come, overtook us both. Without a grin or a smile, we made headways putting on the miles to separate us from such madness. Indio and Yucca Valley came up and so did some relief interrupted by Twenty Nine Palms, or so I thought. We pressed on passing Amboy, Bagdad, Desert Springs, Needles, Kelso Dunes, Kingston Range Wilderness, Mesquite Mountain Wilderness, Old Woman and Pinte Mountain Wilderness. The list went on. Riding and thinking goes hand in hand being my second nature to navigate through all unlike the thinking. We had been on the road three months with much discovery, inner and outer. Spirit a changed dog, closer to me than ever as his eyes never left me and slowly maturing while wondering if I was as well. We were not in the groove yet, that mental easiness one eventually reaches. Every step a bit hesitant even if without much hardship it did not slow us down. I knew this would change with time. A daily practice much becoming second nature, this journey already projecting so many facets in such a short time. It gave me hope life itself would show me the path to enjoy them all.

Have you ever been suddenly elevated through your own senses from your surroundings? Left speechless and at the same time feeling as some gears have disengaged in your train of thoughts while reaching a neutral state of mind? It happened to me unintentionally arriving at Mitchell Caverns. We entered the south side of the Mojave Preserve and Essex Road took us up to the caverns while paying much attention to the road as its uphill hairpin curves demanded such. The scenery came later when stopped in the parking lot. The only and lonely Ranger told us we could camp anywhere. Anywhere? I was in "awe" as I then looked at the valley for the first time, the one we just passed through. It could have probably contained the city of Los Angeles three times over. Breathtaking and more. As we set up camp, I ran out of words and realized my composure had moved beyond the geography, the colors, the peaks and the valleys while already in touch with the spirits wandering. A mental correlation. My inner senses exchanged spaces with each other, a comfortable well being started to take place. The sweetness of the moment took over, recognizing so strongly how much therapy Mother Nature provided. We did not move on for days. It became a habit to go against the grain which pursued me for years when working with a calendar and a watch, mostly the hand of the second mattering. A couple other campers arrived. It was not too social of a space, more of it a retreat with thinking caps on, making room for our illusions of disillusions. We took the tour of the caverns and found myself promoted to Junior Ranger, meaning being the last one of the group turning the lights off as we went along. I gained a little badge from it and the appreciation of the Ranger. As it happened with most caverns, it used to be a silver mine owned by Jack Mitchell and his wife. The mine dries out, it is converted to a resemblance of a Bed and Breakfast for one dollar a night. Jack is killed while working on a car, the caverns are sold to the State. Short version of the story. We woke up freezing one morning and as I looked out the tent, there was snow on the peaks. Absent from any weather news I did not even question the situation. The Ranger asked us to move on before black ice formed on the downhill road taking us back to the valley. We did. What was going to be an overnight stay already turned into a week. Death Valley still resonated in my mind but directions did not matter much anymore, only the weather. The weather which will always be the main factor of the journey. A fact I learned early on. Looking at the map this time, another park attracted me. Joshua Tree National Park.

"Belle", meaning "beautiful" in French, is where we ended up with our own imposing rocks sheltering us. Belle Campground. All natural walls painted in my favorite colors: earth tones. A contact zone as I read a sign not too far away from us. *"It is our tendency to view the Earth as unchanging static. But here engraved upon the face of this mountain is a story of change. The dark mountain is pinto gneiss. The lighter color is granite. The granite crystallized from magna deep within the Earth, which forced its way into the gneiss 85 million years ago. Here, where the two rocks touch, marks the edge of the magna chamber—the contact zone."* And here we were amidst those rocks covering the park, touching each other yet never blending and surrounded by Joshua trees. Magical and eerie all at the same time during the sunsets when they lost their colors and only stood with their odd silhouettes against the darkening skies. We lounged around for the first days within this unusual scenery we were so totally a part of. It became harder to concentrate on a book which could not hold my attention while competing with the present stage. Life as it should be. We were on the right road. I now had no doubt as that "now" more than ever made its definite appearance with a feeling of being on a different planet. The mind had a strange reverberation, thoughts were not taking the path they would normally take. Nature has always been the witness of life going forward, its scenery, its emptiness and at the same time fullness throughout the many years of history preceding us. Timing was everything and still is. I received an e-mail from a good friend of mine, Claude Stanley. A great fabricator of not only sidecars but of a prose I needed to share.

"Where is Home? It is on the road, it is at the small cafe, in the sparkle of our eyes, in the smiles returned, in the sleep on the ground and the pictures painted by the stars above. Life is in the living, life is now. Tomorrow has no guarantees and yesterday has passed. Today is the time of life as all other times are just memories and dreams. Enjoy the day, today is living as living should be. Life is in our hearts as we travel this great land. Worries are few for the chosen few. The ones who have made it a reality to enjoy life for what it can be and what it isn't for so many years are few. We look at others and only wish they were free too. We could only wish they could see, but, they sadly remain blind. Security is so insecure. It creates seeds of worry and concerns over things that in the light of true life are typically trivial and non important. Life is given pleasure that so few experience to its full potential. Life and living are something that we have

learned to define by our own actions. But human definitions are weak and tainted in comparison to what real living can be like. The road, the people, the scenes, defines life of many people for us, but we have to live our own life with what we and we alone make of it. See clearly and be bold for reaching the goal. It is attainable and secure to win but victory comes not just from within. It is our spirituality which has created us, molded us, and can only provide us with true and total satisfaction. Love, Peace and Joy are gifts that have been given and it is only up to us to receive them. Receive them today, as today is the first day and the rest of our life, either on this earth or in another place. Today will be yesterday's tomorrow if tomorrow comes. Today is real, and today is what counts. Yesterdays are numerous, but additional yesterdays cannot be counted on. Today can only be real wherever it is spent and todays are what we make of them. Tomorrow will be affected by our decision made today, but when tomorrow comes, we need to recognize that yesterday has passed. A quandary? For some, for most maybe, but if we make it a point to live today, as if there were no tomorrow, with others in mind, we will be free from these concerns. Pilgrims passing through life? Yes. But it is up to us, and us only, to make those decisions to live life in a way that we bring life to others. By doing this, we are planting seeds in our own life so it can be lived to the fullest. The harvest is great and the investment is small for those who are not blind. Pretty simple really." [Claude Stanley]

So many thoughts, maybe not new but reinforced by the above message. True help and joy dwindling in, smiles, confidence as markers throughout my days, their numbers rising. Another ride through the park with the sun peaking brighter than ever changing the hues surrounding us. The dark rocks gloomier and the granite blanched, cream colored as the contrast surged to its fullest. I will never forget those days and the following ones either as moving on, things did not go so well. It is all part of living on the road, sometimes with no connection for a weather forecast and being at the wrong place at the wrong time. Hole in the Wall, an attractive mysterious name, but not for that time of the year. We arrived into its darkness, a major mistake as ferocious winds picked up, temperatures dropped, a bad night filled with no sleep and the only welcome in the morning came as a thick and damp rolling fog. More layers of clothing. Spirit's coat went on, coffee being made as my hands defrosted a bit while holding them in the mist of the steaming boiling water. I knew this was not going to work out. As much as I don't like putting up a tent for one night, it is what happened. We needed to get out of there before the situation worsened. It appeared to be turning into one of those mornings which teaches many lessons, all left for the mind to always remember. The coffee tasted good while still in the tent but had to soon, while both grumpy, confront the elements to move on towards Lake Havasu. We dropped 2,000 feet in about 15 minutes and right away pulled on the side of the road taking off our layers. I looked at the map, the west side of Highway 95 was closed to the public, lucky us, the east side all BLM land in between Lake Havasu City and Parker Dam. "Surprise me" I said out loud.

We love our BLM land. It is our public land, even if much is slowly changing with oil and gas drilling while some is being leased to private companies. Campgrounds are being built which is a fact not thrilling me. South of Lake Havasu remained untouched and the further we went the more isolation was present. A dirt road to the left, a hill, a couple campers half a mile away. We stopped and made our home in this tropical paradise in deep contrast with the harshness of Hole in the Wall. Time stopped again, no rush. There would not be any moving on for a while, we were still thawing. We went to town the next day. Post Office, provisions and a dog bakery I happened to notice. The treats were expensive, as much as human pastries, but I splurged for Spirit.

He also deserved by then a new pair of goggles, going through them pretty quickly. They are not designed for the daily wear as he does, but they are the only ones made and I bought him a black pair this time. I could barely close the saddlebags and the trunk of the sidecar while riding back. Too much food. We were happy to return, as this time around our borrowed space seemed a good choice. I find campers on BLM land having much more respect than in campgrounds. There are unwritten rules everyone follows. Generators never start early and don't run too late. Everyone is far enough away to barely hear voices, unlike campgrounds where only feet from each other I have always managed to get the drunk in the black truck next to me with the kids screaming, the dogs locked up in their campers and barking all day. This was nice. It was not Joshua Tree National Park, but the weather made up for it. A good friend, Jay, stopped by for a couple nights. That is if you can have friends without having first met them. Yes, we can. Jay had been living on the road for a while. He was the first person I met as such on a motorcycle, and eager to hear his own words of wisdom on the logistics of a life like ours. How to power up our increasingly growing number of electronics, cooking, washing, hygiene, health insurance or the lack of it, maintaining our vehicles, having our mail forwarded. Everything a game changer. Like old friends when he arrived, we tried in our conversations to not cut each other off since we had so much to tell and share. It was time for me to show off my cooking as not too much fun eating alone. A nice rice pilaf with sauteed chicken strips in olive oil, onions, a bit of hot sauce and finished with chopped cilantro, tomatoes and mangoes. That ended the first evening. We went through a second dinner, cooking nonstop while more information, routes and destinations were exchanged. Breaded pork chops topped with a mixture of green onions and more diced tomatoes. A side of a mushroom and herb couscous and some steamed broccoli filled our plates. The store was not very far, quite a convenience when living without refrigeration. We ate better than any establishments nearby and no walls obstruct-ing the scenery, no ceilings hindering the sky's vision, no other patrons next to us and their sometimes not so quiet whispers, all with top notch service. Morning arrived, time for Jay to move on toward his own next destination. We are people lovers, we enjoy the company of others and yet, we are loners. He will be missed and at the same time his solitude on the road again will be gladly embraced.

A recurrence to feel different on the last day at camp while getting ready to move on started emerging. This time not being any different. We could never leave a space seeing and experiencing it all. I invariably thought, rightly so, to leave some for the next time. We jumped on Highway 95 to check out the little town of Oatman. Passed through Lake Havasu City, a short ride on the busy Highway 40 to Topock, and north through the Golden Shores, a stretch of Route 66. The scenery changed to massive younger mountains and many ORV recreation areas which became packed on the weekends. Old Faithful purred as she reached the 170,000 mile marker on her odometer while Spirit born to ride as myself, as always, ecstatic. Such a deep change from the day when I rescued him which seemed so far away, the miles and time building up such a positive aspect towards the both of us. Deserted roads, empty spaces and now in deep contrast, hundreds of people and wild burros all mixed in with some heavy traffic. What was I thinking going to Oatman? The usual tourist traps, the bead stores, saloons, historical buildings barely standing and more burros in the wild. The ones, I heard, that liked to kick dogs as often mistaking them for coyotes. We did not last long, there was no need having seen enough.

Not too far from Kingman, off Highway 93 about four miles east, lies the little town of Chloride. A much better choice, the other side of the coin if such a coin was named Oatman. Again, many historical buildings, but no crowds. A little store doubling as a Welcome Center, a few benches to sit and wait for this world finishing its present spin, an older gentleman driving by to get his daily milk and groceries, a long haired man asking me about a dog found that morning looking exactly like

Spirit while thinking maybe it was mine. The easy life, no worries on those streets, no welcome signs needed. All in the air, free for the taking.

Our first year on the road ended being a bit rough, only because I made it such through my own disregard of likes and dislikes of destinations, compounded with the inability to find, before dark preferably, decent campsites while moving on from what I call "point A to point B". I ignored my likes which were, and still are today, much isolation, empty spaces, "away from it all" and worthy of beautiful photography. A huge country awaiting and probably, most likely, not thinking very clearly on a path where volume competed with the quality of our time spent together, Spirit and Mother Nature, my two companions. I know all of this today, I did not in those times. The doors of this school of life on the road opened up from day one. The bell never rang and the gates have yet to close. A perfect example took place when heading towards Hoover Dam and eventually Las Vegas. I will stop saying "what was I thinking?" Without a doubt, Hoover Dam is a man made wonder with much history, lives sacrificed and the core of more lives for many, enabling them to live with electrical power and creating entertaining spaces around Lake Powell. Unfortunately, not my interest at the time as the road under construction and traffic turned out to be a nightmare. We moved on passing through, managing to admire the construction of this huge cement wall, distracted by the gazillion tourists and their cameras which most of the time pointed at Spirit. My buddy is indeed an attraction. Unintentional for sure. Today, as the years have moved on, many are using their sidecars with the company of their dogs. When the idea originally out of need came to me in years past, I truly believe he was the pioneer of the riding dogs. I will never forget the first ride together. I had learned to maneuver the sidecar without him being a totally different vehicle than a motorcycle, always going right when wanting to go left and vice versa. Ditches were my friends and better off meeting them without him. So there we were all ready, and without a moment of hesitation he jumped in. He let me put on his goggles, which later he would figure out how to take them off himself by shaking his head. His leash attached as I did not have a harness and a helmet yet, and on we rolled towards Dahlonega. Was I surprised? Yes and no! I kept my eyes on the road, at the same time I could not help looking sideways at him. How cool was that I thought. We arrived in Dahlonega, a little town in northern Georgia with maybe three traffic lights at the most, and the strangest thing happened at every stop and when we slowed down. From inside the cars people were pointing and smiling, some laughing as were the ones on the sidewalks. I honestly did not understand for quite a while such behavior. I found it odd. Time went on and I realized it was him, the culprit who to this day has not stopped making people smile and having his photo taken which must be by now on every wall of every home. Probably not, but it sure feels like it. I often ask today to the ones wanting to take a photo of him "What's the matter? You have never seen a dog in a sidecar with goggles and a helmet on?" And 99.99% of the time the reply is no. No one has ever asked if they could take a picture of me. With my back turned I hear too often "Hey good looking...", "Hey cutie...". As a joke, I turn around and say "me?" Of course not. It is constantly about Spirit and forever happy for him.

En route towards Las Vegas. "Towards" the key word as we did bypass the city which wore a brown hat in the form of much smog. We got lost a couple times and ended up camping in nearby Red Rock Canyon without much of a choice. A campground not too bad on the crowd's intensity. We took the self guided tour the next day, and just like tourists do, we stopped at every pull out imaginable admiring the landscape, taking photos and reading the panels for some geological knowledge about how all of this materialized. It said as I learned, that 600 million years ago, the sand which would become Red Rock Canyon, was the bottom of a deep Ocean Basin. About 180 million years ago, a giant sand dune field became the Western United States. Powerful winds shifted the sands back and forth designing its angled lines. Over time, the sheer weight of the layers compressed into stone. The formation known as Aztec Sandstone became quite hard and exposed the present cliffs which caused some of the iron bearing elements to oxidize, a rusting of the sand creating the red, orange and tan present colors. Another short story.

A bad night. Mother Nature and the weather, my mistresses, became more than ever a true revelation, a certitude by then. Destroyed by winds in excess of 70mph mixed with rain, hail and a few snow flurries, the campground looked like a war zone. Most tents flattened or gone, probably downtown Las Vegas by then. Ours stayed up and obviously we both more or less slept through it all. Tunnel tents are designed to handle such times. It was freezing, and as a result we broke camp having to get out of there, find a resemblance of a shelter while never thinking such weather could take place in March this far south. I remembered a Casino a few miles away with a covered parking lot. I begged the attendant to let us regroup for a couple hours with the hope this front would blow over by then. I promised him we were not homeless. A little white lie. I think he took pity on Spirit. Not me. We found a corner where no cars were parked and I unpacked what was shoved into bags in a hurry and repacked the way it should have been, except for the maps needed which stayed out. Having heard of it, Valley of Fire caught my attention. The skies seemed to be resting. I thanked the attendant, hoping he would not get in trouble and on we went arriving a few hours later trying to one more time bypass the city. Free camping became an issue as none existed causing the budget to take a beating. We found ourselves at Arch Rock campground, a jaw dropping site which I definitely thought worth the $14 a night. I called our site the "rock condo". Three walls of red hardened sand surrounded us, and if the winds again picked up we would be well protected. The colors were hues of red, magenta, beige, even yellow and purple. Every square foot had its crevices, odd forms and silhouettes one could give names, all against the skies now blue and nonthreatening. Certainly at one time the campground itself must have been a Native Indian village being so well sheltered from all sides. The photos I took showed the beauty of it all, but none could translate the feelings the rocks were emanating.

We hiked a lot. How could we not. Spirit was off the leash, enjoying every minute of it. Following imaginary lines on the ground like a pointer, he would start to snort when the scents were good. He stopped at times, totally immobile, only his nostrils a bit trembling and ears up. I started doing the same, minus the nostrils and ears of course. It is something I learned from him, instead of saying "let's go", I now wait and can hear the silence taking in deep breaths all along. I found it to be therapeutic and a deep form of meditation within such a conductive space. We saw many arches, silhouettes of a poodle, a frog, honeycombs were everywhere. Little caves served as shelters for us from the sun which by then in full force. I renewed our stay for two more nights trying not to think about the expense. Not using much fuel, one made up for the other.

We moved on to Sedona hearing of much free camping south of town. Having been through the area many years before, the growth amazed me, with again, the eternal road construction and traffic jams highlighted this time by pink colored tour jeeps. I could only think "what a shame having built a city in the middle of this beautiful canyon". It made it impossible to take a photo without an electric pole or line going right through it. We stopped at the BLM office to get the lay of the land and a big disappointment when told not to camp in their space for safety reasons. Hard to believe, such an opulent town filled with posh boutiques and newest models of cars I had never seen, Sedona, the country's capital of meth labs while their addicts roamed the land in search of anything they could steal to sell and buy their drugs. Ending up in Beaver Creek campground its caretakers confirmed such sad truths about the area. Our path was off with such a bad choice of destination while being uncomfortable. Noisy campground, too many people, much commercialism and more traffic. Disappointed, I needed a better knowledge of the country and where to go. I knew it would take some time to learn this without getting impatient. We went to Jerome one day while stopping in mid town to call my Mother. She lived in Munich, Germany. She did not approve of my path and it was my task and responsibility to reassure her all was fine. Another busy little town, which like many, an old mining town. It took us going around and around a few times to find a parking spot. More crowds. I bought some ice cream which compensated the effort, a luxury when one lives without refrigeration. We pushed on to Highway 89 and were rewarded by a beautiful road. The Mingus Mountain Drive, 158 curves in 12 miles. Quite a clearing of the mind and working out the shoulders. Back at camp, destination decision time. How about the South Rim of the Grand Canyon having heard of much free camping in the National Forest, hoping my information was right. For a change!

All true. The best dispersed camping only a few miles from the Canyon, both happy as the choices were great, maybe even with too many of them. Spirit was like a kid jumping up and down as we played among the pine trees. His energy having been bottled up, it finally let go as I watched him so content, both of us reconnecting with Nature and a prevailing silence. I was more excited being there than seeing the Grand Canyon nearby enjoying this home for a few days or as long as we wanted. After we set up camp, everything within me changed. My focus rested on the tree trunks, the ants traveling up and down the half eaten bark, winds howling through the forest. Done playing, I sat on the ground softened by pine needles, my back against a trunk and Spirit lay resting his head on my crossed legs. Just being. Time stopped. No more barriers between Nature and us. Just a forest, greens and browns. No formations, ridges, sandstone silhouettes, hues from the desert colors. Our forest for now, solitude and mental quietness. I began feeling and thinking how much we, as a society, were losing ground on our ability to feel this land from centuries past. It might have been only me thinking as such. Maybe a few others did? The search for vast spaces where the clock and civilization are yet to put their imprint. I know this was my reason for having lived on a sailboat years ago. A spirituality of its own. Dropping the lines and sailing away where nothing being everything. How else would we be able to reconnect with ourselves when haunted by the fear of the fear to really get to know who we are with an awareness that nothing was permanent. The knowledge for us, the fact we will be again at some points throughout this journey in cities for various reasons was well known to me. This space however recharged my batteries which sometimes depleted too quickly, leaving me on an edge of emotions a bit too abrupt. Good things were already surfacing.

We then saw the Grand Canyon. I imagined the expression of the first adventurer coming upon it. It must have been priceless because as one approaches the Canyon, there is no sign whatsoever of the spectacle to be encountered. My only word, as banal as it may seem, was "wow". Huge, a total overload of the senses, a short circuit of the mental fuses. My eyes could not grasp the views and the understanding of Mother Nature's architecture. A humbling experience. Even the crowds did not matter as they fell back, invisible to me. The intensity of the moment made me one with what laid ahead in all three directions like 14 Five Star meal courses all presented at once. We lingered for days on end, every ride towards the canyon a different look out as they never ceased to amaze me. I could never say "I have seen this before".

Time to move. Being by then a few months on the road, Spring in full bloom, summer right around the corner, I was becoming a bit smarter towards our whereabouts, not wanting to get caught in the southern states with a heat increasing by the week. Zion National Park. Without a straight line toward it, not aware of all the treasures which lined the 250 mile route, it was as crossing off names on a list mentally made up. It does not make much sense today, it did at the time. We got around the canyon, Highway 64 eastbound to Highway 89 northbound passing Cameron. Stayed on alternate Highway 89 passing Lee's Ferry and

Marble Canyon, one uneventful night in Kanab and crossed into Zion National Park trying to reach a free campground called Mosquito Cove. The name itself did not sound too good. Just a premonition. Not being summer yet, I thought we would be safe as it did not take a brain surgeon to figure it out. Zion, like the Grand Canyon, became a ten on the scale. There comes a time when one cannot express the "wow factor" anymore without being repetitious. Yet, this park was different. The drama could be touched and walked through. The roads wound around the wonderland always changing. It started raining and could not find my rain pants. I have a map today in my little black book, a map of each bag we carry with its contents. The contents themselves are cross referenced to what bag they are in. I did not have such a map at the time which would have helped locate those pants. I always think it is only water, it dries. We will not melt! The tunnel sheltered us for a few minutes before we were back into the downpour. The rocks glistened wearing a different coat from the water pouring out. Not a good time for sightseeing. We passed Springdale on Highway 9, and between markers 24 and 25 we found the campsites. Its name was worse. Mosquito Cove became Mosquito Landing creating a sarcastic smile. As the weather worsened, I set up quickly, trying to stay as far away as possible from the creek even if at this time of the year the mosquitoes might not be present. The grounds very sandy and having a hard time with my stakes, I found some rocks to keep the guy lines tightened up. Not bad I thought once done. There were a few campers. Perhaps I would strike a conversation with the owner of a well seasoned white van at a later date to learn something from his own experiences. As the weather cleared up, we backtracked for day trips into the park. I heard someone describe it when compared to the Grand Canyon. "You experience the Grand Canyon from the rim, here, you are at the bottom". Well said. Dogs were not allowed on trails and I was disappointed. We so much pay the price because of the few, maybe the many, that do not take care of their dogs, the ones who do not pick up after them. We parked where we could walk along the roads and the flowing waters of the creek. One of those days became mentally hard when watching smiling parents and their beautiful children passing by. Raw emotions surfaced holding back the tears so present. This used to be "us" I kept thinking, the sparks I saw in their eyes missing in mine. I needed to move on, keeping my mind occupied.

Another morning came along and eventually even my toes started warming up. Spirit still asleep wearing two coats and snoring, what a life he has I kept thinking while looking at him. I could have easily traded places as he so totally adapted to his new lifestyle. His dreams at times disturbed me, the ones when he cried. I often woke him up. I knew very little of his first year before I rescued him, only being abused with water. At other times he galloped in his sleep, barking, a faint bark. My own personal show when he would wake me up during the night. We are one for sure. There is not a single aspect of him I would want to change. I never trained him, only built up a mutual understanding through much love and respect, even though he can be so stubborn at times. He thinks he is fooling me by ignoring my words, but I know better. I wait, there is no rush, no schedule. He eventually agrees. Some have argued that building a mutual understanding is as training him. My opinion differs. I love my buddy. What a great companion he has been!

I decided to ride a different route and explore Kolob Terrace Road. Highway 9 westbound to Virgin and head north. Up and up we rolled on and gradually the fields on both sides were covered with snow followed by an intense change in temperature. White blankets mixed in with the rugged mountains, all made me feel as being on a movie set. A sign came up "*No road maintenance beyond this point*". By then, the snow and patches of ice were filling the road. For a couple miles it exited the park and homes appeared with much smoke I could smell rising from their chimneys, obviously with a trace of winter still present at these altitudes. I thought I would not mind a little cabin here as this "was" away from it all, not among the long white buses with their dark tinted windows. No tourists. Blue Springs Reservoir was at the end of the road, but we turned around because Old Faithful's single pusher tire started to spin. Not before we stopped for a long time in a pull out to let Spirit, and I, play in the snow. How much fun was that? Much. I knew he was wondering "what is that?" as I threw some snowballs which he could not catch, and when he did, they would just explode in his mouth.

April 1st came around and Old Faithful had a surprise for me. I wished it would have been an April Fool's joke, but to no avail. On that morning, after only ten feet of riding, I knew something was wrong. And then I saw it. The lower eye bolt holding one of the arms on the sidecar snapped in half. I thought about the positive side. Not far from Springdale which had a welder, this breakage could have happened the day before while negotiating some switchbacks. Happy it broke at camp and not earlier, thankful we were being watched over. I then realized a welder was not going to help the situation. A new eye bolt would. I ordered one right away to be shipped 20 miles from us, and a rider never met before camping not too far from us, offered to go and pick it up. Good Karma? Of course. Again, as it will follow us for the years to come, the big plan hovering over us while everything unraveling according to it. When the part came in at the Post Office, General Delivery, my new friend picked it up and changing it only took minutes. We stayed at camp, I looked at maps planning to visit Bryce Canyon, another name on that imaginary list of mine. A new morning. We were fresh and ready to go when a bicyclist, also a neighboring camper, approached us curious about the sidecar. Bicycles, sidecar mounts, both use very similar tubing welded to each other. As I explained to him the contortion present, his eyebrows rose and I heard him say *"There is a crack in the welding"*. Another arm holding the sidecar had given up. This time the welder needed to help us out. He was not a busy man and we had time as we limped, taking a chance, the 20 miles to Springdale. The tubing itself at the weld joint was cracked and this guy knew his trade. He only asked me one question as he also wanted to reinforce a few other joints. *"Do you want it pretty and painted or do you want it strong and ugly?"* What do you think? So past any cosmetic appearances I said *"Strong and ugly"* of course. He did paint it and is holding to this day.

The repairs completed, we toured Bryce Canyon. One the coldest rides ever climbing at 9,000 feet. Winter in April? Heated gear needed to be hooked up, as in inner jacket and gloves. Spirit's electric blanket and a couple coats were keeping him warm and a day I truly felt like a tourist. Stopping at every pull out, taking a photo seemed like my only mission in this freezing weather. Unhook the electric cords, shoot, hook them back up. I knew we would be back some other time when in warmer weather we could spend a few days. The snow covered hoodoos made up for it all. Majestic, elegant, mixed in, the white and sandstone colors were a sight to see. I did learn much about all these wonders staring at me. Bryce Canyon is actually not a canyon not having been carved by flowing water even though the active ingredient. The process is called "frost wedging". For 200 days out of the year, the temperature consistently varies between above and below freezing. The water melts and seeps into fractures, only to freeze again at night, expanding by 9%. As ice exerts its tremendous force of 2,000 to 20,000 pounds per square inch, over time, this frost wedging shatters and pries the rocks apart. In addition, the rain water which is naturally acidic, slowly dissolves the limestone rounding off the edges and washing away the debris. Bryce Canyon will not last forever with its erosion being one to four feet every 100 years. It is estimated the hoodoos will only last three to four million years. You better hurry up if you have not been there yet. Back again at camp, for the first time, I realized we were slowing down when I found myself thinking we would stay in Utah for another month or so, especially after reading a comment in our journal: *"Chin up. Would you rather be stuck in Utah with a few technical difficulties that will get sorted out, or be solo on a line while the sous-chef and dishwasher call in sick, the Sysco truck shorted your order, the walk in is at 65 degrees, all with a green staff and a line out the front door at 4:55pm?"* "Thank You" for the reminder! Such fond memories.

We made a new friend in Zion. Riders are a bit like magnets, specifically when the motorcycle is the same brand. Parked a few feet from us, a black BMW GS, the rider sitting on a ledge, a conversation ensued. Michael lived north of St George. Married, two dogs, an avid rider, photographer, retired with plenty of time on his hands and a passion for life. He turned out to be a pivotal source in my knowledge of Utah and more in years to come. We talked openly as I generally do, quickly understanding each other's path, coming to the conclusion our meeting was meant to be according to that big plan which always hovers over us. The man knew the roads, the back roads, the trails and best of all, the hidden sights. The ones where the tour buses would not fit. Our conversation turned out to be an introduction to Utah, a short abbreviated version. One which later would have much influence in my love for this State, especially the southern part. He invited us to their home with much hospitality, including our own bedroom, bathroom, and some incredible meals prepared by his wife. What luxury I felt during those coming days! So much so I kept thinking "don't get used to this…". I did not, the call of the wild strong and permanent. Soon after, we rode a few miles north to be shown some BLM land in between two reservoirs where the camping was vast and free. Dreamland. It only took another day or so to move in, off the main sandy road, nicely tucked in between tall trees. Once again exactly what I always looked for. Slowly, ever slowly, the spaces we sought presented themselves to us in a timeless fashion. We rested, relaxed, played some more, I cooked, wrote, we rode a bit, witnessed sunrises and sunsets from the shores of both reservoirs watching the fish jump. Spirit and I lived. One day, a pick up truck with a shell on its bed came by. A man got out, dressed like a fisherman would, waders giving it away. He asked me how the fishing was in the upper reservoir. I told him I did not fish as I could not afford the out of state fishing license fee. Not much else I could tell him besides having watched them jump. I did mention however, that I did know how to cook them having been a chef all my life. He told me to stay there and he would be right back as he walked to his truck and returned with a nice at least 18 inch trout, handing it to me. *"Here, this is for you. It sounds like you will know what to do. I like honest people like you"*, as he reached into his pocket and gave me his card. He was the Game Warden for southern Utah checking up on me. Honesty pays off. I would never fish without a license. What a meal that was!

The good byes were brief. Michael, Sandra and I knew we would see each other again sooner than later. April coming to an end, the timing perfect for Nevada and its vast lands which I thought would only be deserts. Half a year had already gone by filled with the peaks and the valleys of life. A balance in my mind began to take shape comprehending its sway, such being the true fabric of life. Learning slowly but surely. Utah would see us again. Time was not passing us, but us passing by.

The long trek started. This time it really was going to be Death Valley. North on Highway 18 to Beryl Junction and west on 56, which later would turn into Highway 319 past Uvada as we entered Nevada. Then south on Highway 93 at the Lincoln County Airport through Indian Cove and Caliente. We continued west picking up Highway 375 through Tempiute and Warms Springs, arriving in Tonopah, where we turned left southbound on Highway 95 to Beatty, passing through Goldfield. The highlight of it all being the Extra Terrestrial Highway. Just a straight road. One which in the past would have bored me when my riding strictly defined by the "Art of the Twisties". So much changed over time as the moments were a delight. The name itself subconsciously threw in a bit of mystery as one cannot help thinking some alien might appear and? The road gave birth to deep thoughts when stopped at empty intersections where the black top was cut by many dirt roads. Just standing there in the prevailing silence, traffic nonexistent, and here we were all alone on this flat land, a valley surrounded by the distant snow covered peaks of the mountains, the clouds in multitudes of layers, some going faster than others as if in an endless race. Rains must have not been too far as, like a gift for the moment, a beautiful rainbow appeared. If I could only freeze this stage in an eternal memory.

As we fueled up in Beatty, only one mountain pass separated us from Death Valley, a destination so anticipated. The foothills covered with snow from a cold front having just passed through, we stopped when reaching the icy summit, a Ranger blocking the road, a crowd waiting. Lucky for them, Spirit would be their entertainer. The sun, as a giant blow torch slowly took care of the melt down. The downtime gave me a chance to chat with the Death Valley Historical Director who also waited and Spirit stayed too busy being photographed to be bothered. Among much information, the Director assured me our timing was perfect. The bad weather, he said, would be replaced next week, making room for an overnight blooming of wildflowers. I smiled. Finally, the Ranger made the first run down the hill as I wondered, curious me, if he was going to roll or slide. He rolled and it became a go for us as we said our good byes. We set up at Stovewell Pipe campground not quite ready for dispersed camping. The horizons were infinite on this first ride into the park; there was nothing while filled with much, I immediately felt the desolation surrounding us, a fact that will never leave me. From the first hour, a sense of intimidation filtered into my senses. Was it the name? The 3,000 square miles surrounding us? The knowledge of the highest temperature on record reaching 134 degrees? The sunshine disappeared, but came back playing hide and seek. On the following day, the first real all day ride was in order. I could not wait any longer. It turned out to be a bad choice to pick a non-paved road with gravel a foot or more deep. The ground still wet and not hardened, it would remain as such for the days to come. The rear wheel sank in very quickly, a familiar scene as once again we waited for help after a couple futile tries. Jeeps must be our saviors because one showed up and pulled us out. I decided to stay off the unpaved roads, a wise decision for the time being. Be smart, there are 300 miles of paved roads. There were enough to keep us busy for a long time.

"There is something about the desert that doesn't like man, something that mocks his nesting instincts and makes his constructions look feeble and temporary. Yet it's just that inhospitableness that endears the arid rockiness, the places pointy and poisonous, to men looking for its discipline" ~ Blue Highways "William Least Heat-Moon" ~

I have always carried a couple books which filled my soul and showed me a bit of the path we were taking. They are about others who preceded us putting into words so eloquently our own experiences, "Blue Highways" being one of those books. Death Valley was a real desert, nothing to be fooled with. One could be found being alone for days on end. Every morning a ritual became essential. Double checking the rig, tire pressure, making sure we indeed had spare tubes, patch kits, the compressor working, the spare quick start battery full, solar batteries, our live GPS tracker [SPOT] operational, plenty of water and food, thermal blanket, extra fuel and oil, first aid kit and the list went on. It turned out I used most to rescue others who still thought they were driving or riding in downtown Los Angeles. There was no AAA present as many might have believed. The word "survival" made its presence more often than not as eventually we reached desolate destinations, camping spaces commonly called dispersed and primitive. Overpowering substances within my own layers of contemplation throughout this convergence aimed at all my senses. Death Valley did not procure me with much rest. I always felt as being on a sailboat about 100 miles away from shore, with a constant attentive mind towards what would keep us alive. At the same time, as lying down and surrendering to this artistry present, my fascination heightened by the day. I wanted to set roots within each of those spaces we experienced with the incredible quality preceding the overwhelming quantity.

We made it to the Racetrack. A thoughtless day throughout the third sun passing over us. Could it really have been a thoughtless day? The shade cold and in plain view the sun hot. Spirit did not seem to think so while working on his suntan. The flowers had been blooming. The man was right. Progressively the reflections of my life infiltrated my thoughts, they could not stay still for too long having taken years to get there. The space so generous and at the same time dominant. I felt it so strongly as a last frontier before passing through another gate towards this world of ours, the past dark abyss finally not as dark as it used to be. Even though some lookers were passing by on their day run, I created this fantasy that we are alone. Only curious are the others. Our lifestyle is for us different, with longer moments than theirs savoring these days so countless of time not present. The skies remained a plain unobstructed blue, not a good background for photos, but the images were now imprinted in my own soul. The fragmented floor of the Racetrack shone and deepened its wrinkles looking like a giant puzzle. Not a single piece the same, yet, all so perfect. How about if all were scrapped and put in a box? Could humans put it all back as is? Laid out so properly? I did not think so. Only Mother Nature could accomplish such a task. I achieved a more stabilized balance. The few rocks on the La Playa reminded me of my own mental ones. They moved throughout the storms when windy and flooded under much darkness from the skies. They rested throughout the good weather as we did. No walls surrounded La Playa and when a storm hit, we had front row seats. The lightning struck with no boundaries and thunder with its infinite echo. Walls and I don't get along very well. The days passed as my own roots dug in deeper. Sometimes the quest becomes questionable fueled by the complexity of this human mind. Dreams of sharing appeared. Sharing with Lance would be the ultimate and yet, a bittersweet thought. We would not be there if Lance had still been alive. This was his gift handed over with a generosity unlike any others. An acquired wealth now shared through my own written words emanating from this nomadic life we embraced with a steep price, one willing and always ready to pay. One so considerable I bowed to without looking back, as even if I did, the key of the past life mode became lost not to be found. Heaven seemed to be under our feet as well as over our heads.

The days spent in the vicinity of the Racetrack took me back to my raw lineage. Overwhelmed, we left with a handy map strapped to my tank bag. Oddly enough I felt ready to play tourist for a while. See others. Stovepipe Wells too urban, Panamint campground would do. Quieter, privately owned and reasonable fees. Only for a couple nights until I found another empty space within those three million acres. As we settled, I pulled names from the map. It did not matter which won that day being our first time in Death Valley. With no doubt, we would return throughout the coming years. Ubehebe Crater, the nice hike in Mosaic Canyon, Mesquite Flat Sand Dunes, Salt Creek, Harmony Borax, the stunning panorama of the Badlands from Zabriskie Point, the three unpaved miles of the one way Twenty Mules Canyon, Artist's Drive, the cone headed Charcoal Kilns, Badwater Basin, Dante's View. We rode Titus Canyon, admired Scotty's Castle. The rest and more would have to wait. Summer began making its presence felt. It was time for us to head north for a few months.

A city not too far. Its name kept playing in my mind, tapping on my shoulder and hiding at other times through a mental game. San Francisco. A tough call, a one act play to relive happy and painful times seeing it as a personal challenge. I knew that is where we would end up very shortly, as much as I kept wondering why I wanted to put myself through such emotions being the stage where Lance and I spent many years together. I needed to confront such a play scene by scene, where this time around I would be the spectator lost in the audience, when instead I used to be one of the actors. I needed to get around this bend ahead of me where darkness resided and try to lighten it up by genuinely looking into my mirror. Life, I was learning, never meant to be easy. Some facts were harder to handle than others, its harshness could only make someone stronger even if the bridge crossed did not allow for much balance. We started heading that way. Picked up Highway 395 northbound in California, passing Bishop on the way to Mono Lake, where before Lee Vining we would pick up the same Highway westbound which would take us through Yosemite National Park. We called some friends in nearby Sacramento whom I thought we could perhaps stay with and take day trips for as long as needed to San Francisco. We connected but the plans changed. We were going to stay in Cupertino instead, camp in the backyard of John and Carol's home, friends we had yet to meet. My interest for Yosemite expanded, a familiar park while living in the Bay Area. Its grandeur always amazing me as another natural wonder in sight. This time, I had to put up with the tourists in roofless buses and cameras swayed toward Spirit to no end. The quality of the roads also changed. Potholes, cracks and even craters having to pay much attention if I did not want to bend a rim, something already done in years past. The city played on my mind more than anything else, as well as a heavy heart unable to live in the present moments because of too much anticipation towards the times to come. The GPS took us to Cupertino, and there it was, the last one on a cul-de-sac, John and Carol's house. Both great hosts and dog lovers, they had just lost their own and Spirit was for them a welcomed visitor. The next day, we took our first ride into the city. I waited a while for the early commute to lighten up, heaved a big sigh, and we rolled onto the freeways still busy even past rush hour.

San Francisco. A city familiar to me as it was to Lance. His backyard, one of the loves of his life, unlike me, a city young man. Restaurants, many friends, entertainment, the busy life, nice fashionable clothes, a magnetism reverberated by an incredible constant energy never lacking. We arrived under perfect weather and made a loop taking the shoreline stopping at Washington Park in North Beach. The Italian neighborhood, the one with the many benches this time around not occupied by us, but by strangers. I tried to close the doors of my emotions to separate the past from the present while deep down I knew it was not possible. I went in not quite knowing how I would really feel. I saw Lance everywhere. The little cafes where we would go sit for hours watching the crowds pass by, this restaurant and that one entering early on his insistence for better food and service. I saw that same bench where just being, we felt the world around us go by while I watched his own expressions always thinking of it as magic to have such a son. I felt numb. As much as I believed the city tried to embrace me with open arms, there lingered this emptiness as I knew she would never show herself as a full glass. I was however glad to be there. It provided the closest presence to him I would ever feel. We moved on a bit further, watched Alcatraz and the boat traffic while we sat on the Greens where the frisbees and kites flew as always. What a memory lane. I did not belong to the space anymore as I once had. The Oakland Bay and the Golden Gate Bridges, both still there. I remembered Lance and I riding our bicycles over the Golden Gate Bridge, dropping down to Sausalito and coming back on the ferry. What wonderful remembrances. Lucky me to have had the opportunity spending those years with him even if shortened in their span. I looked at the bright side, at that glass which would always remain half full and not half empty. Those past years in the city were filled with so much love and still blind toward the tragic events that were to follow. Life is so unpredictable, there are no reruns, no second chances, it is not a rehearsal as the play goes on. Spirit, quiet all day, I knew he felt my inner battle, I had no doubt about it. Dogs, especially when as close as he and I are, have such an incredible sense. I knew he read me well. He never met Lance, but who knows, maybe he understood the present. I felt bad for him also going through such emotions, yet it is the core of partnerships. To be there for each other through thick and thin.

The week ended up being one of a different fabric from any other experience throughout our journey. It has never been duplicated. I moved on to another window and looked through it at our present and recent past path able to regroup, as I will use that word often in years to come. There were some new conclusions and reaffirmations having met so many wonderful people. I remembered leaving on this journey the both of us alone, we were not anymore. Carol and John could not have been nicer or more considerate towards our needs and stay. The other side of the coin was my surroundings having thrown me off balance, wishing for better past scenarios, future ones, so totally unable to plant myself in the present as hard as I tried. The air was slowly being sucked out of my space, the lid getting tighter due to not only Lance's memory, but longing what we experienced, such as the Racetrack not long ago.

Time for good byes with Carol and John. We headed north following the coastline of California. A destination given to us by another new friend. The name itself intriguing and promising. California Lost Coast. Its description portrayed a likable space and ambiance, a serenity much needed after our urban stay. We passed Santa Rosa, where Lance was born, Willits, Rio Dell, Fortuna, missed our turnoff and ended up in Eureka. Traffic became scarce, Highway 101 turned into a two lane road seeing more motorcycles than cars due to the "Redwood Run" happening that weekend. Much waving. While passing the Avenue of the Giants, long stretches on both sides of the road turned greener from the waters of the French Broad River with fields of grapes and wineries taking up hundreds of acres. No loss while in Eureka. After some grocery shopping and refueling, we turned around to take the northern approach of the Lost Coast, which by now according to the map was south of us. Mattole Road through Ferndale, an old quaint Victorian style little town, Capetown, and the road turned out to be a really bad broken up one. Steep uphills and downhills with hairpin turns. The flowers were in bloom, the ocean lost its blue color mixed with the fog rolling in from north of us, now becoming a grayish surface, a new canvas. We rode right along the ocean with its endless horizon, a bit of a humid breeze and the smell of sea salt. A good prescription. I found the turn off and there we were, once again falling in love, maybe even in lust, with another space. A small BLM campground, twelve sites or so in a circle separated from the beach by only a sand dune. There were a few other campers, obviously not being the only one in search of such space. I set up quickly as by now a routine to do so. I kept Spirit on his long leash for a short while as we walked onto the beach and set him free. The roar of the surf, the waves breaking on the hardened sand so loud sometimes sounding as a train passing by, my whole body, mind and soul let go of any tension built up from the past week. This, now real. As the days went on with no clock or calendar, we both spent most of our time sitting on the many larger drift woods present, just being. We watched the shadow of a giant sun dial someone built slowly move in deep contrast from us so still. The campground had a different atmosphere from any other we experienced. No one was there to be loud, even talk to each other. It felt like being in a space for a retreat and happy about that. Back on the beach, the ocean appeared as a giant avenue. It made me feel so small in comparison to its vastness. We laid down on dark nights and watched the stars play while myself feeling smaller and smaller. Life played on that ocean. More questions arose, few answers came through. It did not matter. Spirit and I were together within again another slice of heaven.

Witnessing our last sunset confronted by this ocean while on the beaches of the Lost Coast took place. We needed to leave the next morning. One more new friend, an ex-BMW master mechanic, offered to take Old Faithful apart and redo the mounts, beefing them up with new reinforced plates and more. How could I say no as already headed his way north to cooler weather. The last sunset turned out to be the most fascinating one ever watched. The location could not have been a better stage in total harmony between land, water, sounds, smells and my buddy tucked in next to me. I felt we had come a long way and could with just a thought, fly away, walk on water, so much more. Silly me sometimes. I took a polished stone with me as a memory besides what was parked up there in my head. We left on the southern route. The one which goes through Petrolia and had missed on our way up. It took us among the Giants, that would be the giant trees, on a road just as bad if not worse. There were no complaints though. Well worth it and maybe a good thing as it kept the crowds away. The sun setting when we entered Humboldt State Park on Bull Creek Road, everywhere I looked, the brown bark was covered with the greenest moss and I could not see the tips of the trees. The road barely made it between some of the trunks at times not spaced out far enough from each other. Too bad we could not have camped there for a few days. We needed to move on. I could not miss Andy's offer made during his vacation. Such a kind gesture.

Highway 101 north. A never ending road lined with crowded beaches as the campers on the weekend were in big numbers, everyone a couple feet from each other. They could probably smell each other's cooking, hear every word spoken, maybe even the snoring of their neighbors. On the sand dunes, the little quads were buzzing at warp speeds with their high whipping antennas and their red flags. "Keep moving" I thought. All the beaches were alike through Trinidad at College Cove Beach, Patrick's Point State Park, Dry Lagoon Beach, Del Norte Coast Redwood Park. We passed by Crescent City and landed in Oregon. A quick night without a choice at the Pistol River State Park, and again the wheels turned the next morning. We passed by Oregon Dunes National Recreation Area and it felt as the whole country had taken refuge on those beaches. I could not blame them though. Everyone has the right to enjoy the outdoors the best they can. Those areas are designed to handle such crowds. I mellowed out within my thoughts. "Raise your respect level" I told myself, we are all different. I needed a better handle on the gray areas of our life.

Under dark forecast skies, along with some drizzle and cooler temperatures, we pulled in at Andy's house near Enemclaw, Washington. One away from the hustle and bustle of an urban setting, a farm-like picture with horses, a couple dogs, wife and kids. Much room to camp and of course a garage. I felt Andy's energy and passion for working in his shop, as maybe being retired from his past profession he missed it. He wanted to look over the motorcycle itself, and without waiting much longer, he took it for a test ride returning with a thumbs up. After checking some linkage, the transmission which we thought could have been an issue, was fine. Too fast for me, I could not even hand him the tools as they appeared like magic in his hands, and kind enough to say "we" have been working on Old Faithful, as mostly I just stood there and watched learning much. The shocks came quickly off to be sent away. They were to be rebuilt as one of the seals leaked. The sway bar would need to be addressed, the car realigned along with much sanding, priming and painting. Some mechanical maintenance such as a new belt, fuel filter, brake fluids, all to be changed. Adjust the valves, rocker arms, throttle bodies and a few other parts. With 170,000 miles on her and a long life ahead, Old Faithful needed such care. The sidecar detached, custom designed reinforcements were added on, welded, painted. All modifications I felt the manufacturer should have thought about. My excitement rose to a new level. One morning as I took my first steps of the day, I noticed the garage door closed. Maybe Andy worked late the previous night while I slept being of no help at all. He appeared with a strange look on his face and asked me if ready for this? For what? Don't get excited he said as he opened the garage door, and the motorcycle itself laid totally apart as never seen before. My heart skipped a beat but he reminded me, seeing my own expression "Remember, I am a Master Mechanic...". So what happened? He felt like getting deeper into the heart of it. The engine still held in one piece, but nothing else seemed to be. To this day I don't exactly know what he did, but Old Faithful went on for another 100,000 miles before blowing its engine. So many "Thank You's". The company and the space were good, and when the shocks returned, we were prepared to go. Go where?

The ride felt brand new. The suspension, power, smoothness, shifting and above all, the confidence in the strength of the arms holding the sidecar, Spirit's car, my buddy ready as much as I to take off leaving behind much play time with Andy's dogs and chasing the horses a couple times too many. He now seemed content back in his car. Mount Rainier ahead of us, we could not leave the area without experiencing this volcanic mountain covered with snow and a peak reaching 14,410 feet. Beautiful ride on Highway 410 along the Green River, a slight right on Sunrise Road and the road stopped at an elevation of

6,400 feet. The Sunrise Visitor Center surprised me with the amount of snow left at such time of the year and low altitude. Once more we played, and the snowballs a must. Time passed, we needed to search for a new home, one among Nature where we could spend some downtime and regroup. The map came out and I picked the Olympic Peninsula not too far from us, trying to figure out a route which would avoid Seattle, meaning much traffic. We set out enroute for Olympia riding familiar Highway 101, leaving the outcome in the hands of chance. The Peninsula welcomed us with cool weather totally escaping the heat of summer. A good choice, no doubt. I felt so good being off the mainland, all with a laid back and relaxed atmosphere, inviting even if still without a clue towards a space to live. We came across a resort, one of those low key dwellings with no pretense where I stopped hoping I would be able to get some information. A quarter mile away, they owned a quiet piece of land barely off the road where one could set up for a slight overnight fee. Exactly what we needed. As we set up and the days went on, I discovered the most valuable motorcycle after market item we would need day in and day out. Rain gear. We both had it, Spirit needing his cover daily as the rain or a constant drizzle would not stop. We took a ride to Lake Cushman, an area with many unpaved roads making circles of different diameters all around the Peninsula. The rain spared us some days but a thick fog always present. I knew that anywhere else summer would be in full force and we never did very well around heat. With many children, a Vietnamese family moved in a couple hundred feet from us. Their pots and pans came out and quietly, with much respect, they went on doing their daily chores and oyster picking on the beach across the road. They knew what they were doing since being a yearly outing for them. Vietnamese meant for me that perhaps they spoke French. They did, as I approached them tagging Spirit along on his leash. Instant friendship, food, strong coffee and the kids all wanted to sit in the sidecar under the concerned eyes of Spirit! Many smiles and photos. This is what life on the road is all about. Meeting others from all different walks of life. Sharing conversations, eating together, laughing and the children playing. Good times.

Big news while looking at the weather forecast, an appearance of the sun! Everything surrounding us had been for days in hues of grays. We might start seeing real colors. Sure enough, we did and climbed aboard heading towards Port Angeles where we made a left on Hurricane Ridge Road then all the way to Lake Mills where the thick forests, cool, damp and beautiful felt so comfortable. Even thought maybe we should move and camp out there, but for more than one reason, we were comfortable and I did not mind the couple dollars a night which provided showers a quarter mile away. The day ending up being so exceptional, I decided we should ride the complete Peninsula loop a couple days later. Three hundred fifty miles was not a long day by my old standards when on two wheels I could easily average 800 miles, on other days the magic number of 1,000. Sometimes these days I feel lucky we are not going backwards instead. I remembered one day near Sacramento when we rode 12 miles in ten hours taking it all in while taking too many photos and much time for us to stretch. So many changes over the years. Done with the 100+ mph days, now the speed mostly cut in half. I liked it that way. Time is all we had.

I finally took off the sidecar windshield. Spirit kept rubbing his nose against it and the delicate skin starting to peel off. His goggles, coats, cover and heated blanket when needed would be enough protection. I later found out my fuel consumption gained close to five miles to the gallon. We moved on, away from the familiar Highway 101 previously ridden to Port Angeles and picked up the deserted Highway 112 following the Strait of Juan de Fuca. A beautiful ride, a gorgeous day as we passed Clallam Bay entering Makah Indian Reservation arriving in Neah Bay, the most northwestern point of the country. Small town of only a couple square miles with less than a population of 1,000. The air the cleanest and friendly locals. Time seemed to have stopped, no one going anywhere, everyone already there, here. A small harbor with fishing boats not yet gone out, the smallest school building ever seen, and at some point more locals coming out smiling when seeing Spirit in his chair. Afternoon rolled around a bit faster than I preferred, we could have sat on that beach forever but needed to go on finishing the loop. I wished we had brought our camping gear when on the return route I saw some inviting campsites right on the water where Highway 101 turns into the Pacific Coast Scenic Byway as Abbey Island appeared. Further south, the coastline took on many names stopping often for photos, the sun slowly setting, colors changing from their daytime harshness to their golden hues, all so desirable. Closer to Olympia an impression of urbanism showed its face and our campsite awaited. It was an evening of peanut butter and jelly being too tired to cook, or maybe I did not want to bother with dinner. Hard to believe, we had been there for two weeks.

I thought about going east to the Columbia River and on to the High Deserts of Oregon. For sure Spirit would not mind. As always, I felt apprehensive when leaving an area in which we fit so nicely and connected with so well. Simultaneously, pure adrenaline rush set my eyes on new territories. I could not figure the dilemma of too much freedom. Maybe we just needed to rest some more, but taking roots was not comprehensible either. Instead, I went with the flow, leaving behind much we could experience another time, a good excuse to come back. We dropped to Portland. The city slapped me with its traffic, congestion and pollution. What was I expecting? This would be a corridor leading us to better spaces. We rode State Road 14 along the Hood River which reminded me many times we were in "Lewis and Clark" country. The white caps noticed on the river were increasing and around one bend I saw dozens of wind surfers. We stopped for the entertainment, a water break, more photos. We were between point A and point B, waiting for point B to materialize for the night, who knows, maybe again for days. As we pushed east toward the Oregon High Desert, we came upon Baker

City and stopped at the Oregon Trail Interpretive Center. What luck! I started to feel I was imitating Spirit with also a good nose.

In the Center, we met a wonderful lady named Pauli who gave me much information about Hell's Canyon including directions to many free campsites. It turned out she was the one who actually designed the recreation area. With map in hand, I knew exactly where to go. As much as I wanted to walk around and learn a bit of history about the Pioneers and their past trails, the day getting late, we took to the road again. We would come back at a later date. With quite a distance to go, but on the right track, Richland appeared, Halfway, and finally Oxbum with its bridge and Idaho on the other side. A nice gravel road while we made a left before the crossing, rode through a tunnel carved in the mountain, and the campsites appeared. It was very late by then, warm and hazy. I wondered why? I just threw down the sleeping pad and bag and sleep came quickly that night with Spirit curled up next to me.

The first rays of sunshine woke me up with my throat a bit raspy and a warmth in the air already in the higher digits. Beautiful campsites. Waterless bathrooms, flat spots for tents, some trees for shade and the sight of the Snake River running close by. Yet, quite a haze in the air and I realized, feeling ignorant from the night before, there must be a fire in the area. Not what we needed. I didn't set up camp, only repacked my pad and bag and headed back to Oxbum, just a few miles away to find out about the fire or what could be fires. It did not take too long while chatting with a local, to hear that a fire came through the Canyon and burned 70,000 acres. Was I blind to the remains? It had not burned it all and the roads reopened only a couple days earlier. It left me a bit dumbfounded wondering why none of it mentioned when meeting that nice lady named Pauli. So now what? In love with the area, but not with the haze and the temperature, I understood the meaning of its name, Hell's Canyon. We were in August, mid-summer, having escaped the heat, now right back into it. I became hungry but remained patient.

They both went hand in hand, it is a must. The same local told me about a little restaurant in Halfway which served good food. I went for it trying to regroup and figure out what to do, where we would stay. Decent restaurant, they tried a bit too hard as the food looked better than it tasted. Fine with me, I made the price worthy with some extra bread and butter. Water also. There are a few things one learns on the road. The use of public restrooms, with their soap and hot water being priority, never letting the opportunity pass me by. The other while eating out, to receive as much as possible for the least amount of money, and that included drinking water. So much we took for granted in the past, now luxuries. Done with the meal I waited for the magic which materialized soon after while spinning around Halfway.

I noticed a resemblance of a motel next to the town's arena. Across the road from it, about 500 feet towards the end of town, I remembered seeing a campground with a couple RVs and a couple tents. I found out both having the same owner when I stopped at the motel's office to inquire. It seemed quiet, the temperatures were cooler than in Hell's Canyon and town not too far. We could walk to it if necessary. Where else would we want to be in the middle of summer? Montana and Wyoming were not yet on my maps. With a weekly and monthly rate, two weeks being the same price as a month, I did not think about it too long. Getting a bit edgy about having a place to rest for a while, longer than we normally did, the decision which I never regretted, one month. As before, we would cut back on fuel money and use our feet.

Sometimes I have found myself staring at the right knob throughout this journey. With a little twist of the mind, a door opens as I fall right into its present moment, without a past or future. It is a space where no decisions are needed, where one "is" and can "be". A landing where a mirror-like reflection of life keeps the ripples away. Mental fonts start creating paragraphs as the mind does not stand still too long, especially after reading an e-mail I received *"I am just a guy with two raw nerves*

*rubbing together, his heart on his sleeve, all potential and no direction,
naked in the face of his fears and his peers. I love and I am loved, in some
ways. Sooner or later, it is all going to come together and my money is on
magic. One of these days…".*

All set up, having a hard time believing we would be there for a month,
I sat calmly in my chair staring at the skies passing by trying to never
forget the magic, the fascination which had already taken place and
appeared in such fortunate times when taking a wrong turn, putting us
on the right road. Not alone anymore, words from many others made
their way into our lives. It became the icing on the cake. Quite often
the cake itself. A first for us, in a mildly mannered way, to be part of
a community. We discovered the Saturday morning organic farmers
market, having to show up early if I wanted some of those nicely per-
fumed little wild strawberries, fresh potatoes being wiped down by the
man's T-shirt, basil one could smell from five feet away, the sweetest
onions ever tasted, fresh baked goods and so much more. How about
a fresh warm maple roll while sitting on a bench enjoying a steaming
cup of coffee and simply chatting. We stumbled on an organic peach
orchard in Richland a few miles away. From peaches, to apples, pears
and prunes, many acres of them. I bought the bruised peaches at half
the price, all stuffed in a bag. All the fruit and vegetables tasted as they
should, as they did a quarter of a century ago. While I cooked a lot, if
I remember well, with all the fresh produce around I ended up never
eating any meat. There was no need for it.

We did not just exist in Halfway but started living. With much going
on in town we made it into a real base camp. I wanted to be part of it all
with the welcoming and friendly locals. A new concept in our journey.
The map showed so many rides. Some into the forests of Hell's Canyon
Recreation Area, some along the Snake River and one more favorite. After
crossing the bridge in Oxbum, heading to the dam but making a sharp
right and up into the mountain, Kleinschmidt Grade through Payette

National Forest. We took rides to Cornucopia. A ghost town close to the Idaho border off Highway 86 in Wallowa-Whitman National Forest. Discovered in 1884, I read that the gold ore was so rich, nuggets would just fall out of the rocks. Many buildings still standing as we parked on Main Street hearing the voices coming through the swinging doors of the saloons, carriages rolling in and out of town, I even heard some gunfights, laughter and some cries. As mentioned, Kleinschmidt Grade a favorite. A road with many switchbacks and built straight up into the mountain looking menacing from the start. After making it to the top, we came to a little town called Cuprum, established in 1909, elevation of 4,276 feet and population of 12. We did not see a soul as we parked and just stood there a bit baffled. The roads went east almost indefinitely, miles of no man's land. It took a few hours to arrive in Council where I treated myself with a slice of coconut pie and a cup of coffee. Highway 95 welcomed us with traffic. Highway 71, a bit further south in Cambridge, turned out to be the opposite all the way back to Oxbum and eventually back to camp. More riding and loops the coming days as much as we ended up not adventuring out as often while resting and just living. From Richland, we took Snake River Road, another magical ride along the water all the way to Nagle and Huntington, a few miles of Highway 84 and somehow made it back through Lookout Mountain Road, more by sheer luck than anything else as those roads were not on my GPS. That little gadget only slightly larger than a stamp. I was glad having overlooked the signs which said "*Caution, sharp curves, falling rocks and severe slides for the next 38 miles...*". It became a common surprise when in the many evenings we rolled back to camp to find produce dropped off by the locals. Homegrown tomatoes, cucumbers, the sweetest corn ever tasted, zucchinis, squash, green beans and fruit. I often did not know who dropped them off. I would find out later while in town when someone would ask me " Did you enjoy the produce?" Of course... of course... and many thank yous.

I heard the big news one day. A rodeo coming to town, a yearly event. Never having attended one, I did not know much about them except what one sees in the movies. A few readers of our journal wrote advising me to move on as thinking, from what I am sure was their own personal taste, I would not enjoy it. We were not going to move, I instead looked forward to the new upcoming experience. Within walking distance, I could even leave "poor" Spirit behind. Someone brought me the program one morning. Free breakfasts, each provided by different sponsors, watermelon seed spitting contest, vegetable costume competition, photography and baking awards. I would attend them all including much of the riding and a lot more. The local baker, the same one selling her goods every Saturday at the farmers market, stopped by. She asked me if I could do some baking as she was not up against anyone else. She wanted a bit of friendly competition. I turned her down, the logistics just too difficult while camping. We waited and slowly the town started seeing more traffic, banners went up and the campground saw many move in. We were lucky, we did not have to move out, only a couple spaces over since all reservations for that weekend were made a year in advance.

While waiting, the twists and turns of the journey unraveled in my mind those days. How much I loved my Mother even if physically so distant living in Germany, Spirit, my buddy with a heart of gold, Mother Nature and her canvases forever changing and spoiling my senses, my friends, good food and myself, as I tried so hard to, yes, love myself. Everyone needs to love themselves. I found it to be a must to cope with the poundings life can procure. The volume up from all those knobs while at the same time so much missing Lance with the deep appreciation of his gift. I could have never thrown in the towel at this point, not a feasible concept while enjoying our freedom to roam, learning the valuable lessons on how to live on the road and the indulgence of emotions so new to me. They ran loose not being held back, no reason they should have been. Rooted deeper they lingered longer, expanding to their fullest. I had so much more spiritually and so much less in material possessions. A good trade off.

The rodeo arrived. To be more exact, the "Baker County Fair and Rodeo". Such a totally different crowd, all the way to how they dressed. Some cowboy boots and hat I thought would be very cool only if I could learn the "walk". But where would I carry them? It turned out to be a welcomed family and children experience. With their five children and goat, the Croomers moved in next to us. All five young ones home schooled, all showing livestock as they also had a cow somewhere by the arena. They taught me much I did not know. There were sheep, turkeys, lambs, pigs and chickens, an impressive experience. They invited me to share their meals, since as curious towards our lifestyle as I was of their's. The last day of the fair all the animals were sold at auction to help out with the children's educations. What a great program. One big family affair while grooming, cleaning, washing, brushing and sometimes as I witnessed, painting the hoofs of cows. All together, a "feel good" experience. How refreshing not seeing a single child with a Nintendo game or a smart phone. Only a few feet separated the fair from the actual rodeo in the arena. Abundance of food, home made pies and ice cream, fried this and that, BBQ. No quads or bicycles present, everyone rode a horse, including children three feet tall, sometimes up to four of them on one horse. These were days glad having left Spirit behind because of all the present commotion. The main parade took place, followed by the "critters costume contest". None were about the fair or rodeo anymore, but about the unity I felt among the many families present and the future generation. The rodeo turned out to be an amazing display of bull riding, roping, barrel racing, children riding lambs, calf roping, goat tying, steer roping, bareback riding and so much more past sunset when the lights came on. Also time for the carnival and the rides, all in brightly lit multicolor neon. Amazing days.

The last horse trailer left, the carnival disassembled, the dust laid back on the ground undisturbed. September arrived with a coolness felt in the air. We were going back to Texas, maps in hand trying to decipher which route to take. "Why?" I finally asked myself. Did it really matter?

I faced the concept of adventure instead and back the maps went into the tank bag, neatly folded, stored away. Yet, we could not leave and extended at a special price our stay for another week. Little bacterias anonymously decided to camp out in my throat for the following days having built a fire and roasting marshmallows. I wished they had not taken a hike into my brain and left it hurting from the heat. The days felt as the frames of a movie called "Campfire" while moving in slow motion with every gear scraping and scratching the celluloid with each pass. It eventually become a memory. We left Halfway filled with emotions. Where else would the hardware store attendant come out for a good bye hug? Where else would everything which took place happen again? It never does, never quite the same way.

Through the eastern parts of California, we ran away from the changing weather, fall present and winter not too far behind. I unpacked the heated gear for both of us. Big Bend became the only name dancing in my mind while the miles unraveled day after day through Sacramento, Bakersfield, Kingman, Phoenix and Tucson for the final 600 mile stretch through El Paso to our destination. We arrived back at Terlingua in mid-day, for some reason totally off balance. Were there too many expectations? And if so, what were they? I did not know while the both of us so tired. I knew I would never do that drop again from north to south in such a quick time. Just a few days. We needed some rest.

Too tired to get into the park, we stayed at the same campground as before. I could call my Mother from the only pay phone in town and stay in touch with friends. Terlingua had at the time, two gas stations and two grocery stores, today down to one each. An e-mail arrived from friends living 30 miles up the road, asking me if I would be interested in buying ten acres of land. All weather accessible, about 25 miles north of Terlingua, a couple miles off Highway 118. The price? $150 an acre. It had not even been a year since we left Georgia. Land. Land now? Wanting to see it we arranged a ride while a bit excited about it. More curious than anything else and already thinking, "our own campsite"? A left on a dirt road, one more, and a stunning landscape appeared. Not a single dwelling in sight. The western horizon ahead of me, untouched it seemed by human hands, behind stood Nine Points, a mountain with appreciable height, more hills south, an open vision to the north. With no idea how big ten acres would be, we tried to figure it out by walking paces. All flat terrain, it seemed immense. The parcel next to it also for sale but a bit hilly. I did not care for it. Yes, I fell in love with the space in an instant. I could see us spending our winters right here with a little town such as Terlingua not too far. Emotional, as we left returning to camp, a huge decision faced me, or had I already answered myself? Yes. The vibes felt good. I would worry about water and power later on as everyone else around here. Only a slight handicap, I did not have the money to buy it. Back to the phone booth and after a long conversation with my Mother, she would buy it for us. A Christmas present as she called it at the time, even though she did not understand why I would want to live as such during winter times in the middle of nowhere with no running water or electricity. We were learning to agree to disagree. Such changes had been huge steps in our lives, in our friendship and relationship. I had a very cool Mother. We returned a couple days later, this time with a measuring tape and figured out exactly its boundaries. No reason to pay someone to have it surveyed, there was no one else around within miles. The paperwork did not take long and soon after we left the campground and spent our first night on what I call to this day "The Oasis". I started more schooling on how to truly live as they say "off the grid". Having lived as such for almost a year, it would not be difficult, I thought at the time.

An intense first night, as poignant as it still always is when we return for these winter times. The definition of silence, only broken by the coyotes from right to left and vice versa, the packs finally joining. A sky with no moon or light pollution while lying down to look up, slowly intensifying which with time would be lit instead of dark from so many stars above as a blanket protecting us. The cold in the morning would drop as the heat rose with the sun emerging from behind Nine Points. I had overlooked the only one Mesquite tree present which has now grown a few feet. Creosote and cactuses lined up at every step. It was magic and still is.

The journey would not come to a halt. I considered this place being another base camp in our lives, and as the days went on, we started exploring the three million acres surrounding us. Our land, ten acres at 3,500 feet. I could not get over the concept. Rolling into Terlingua, as familiar as it was, it all looked new, already seeing and sensing my surroundings with a sharpness non-existent before. We hang out in town often, welcomed by many, unwelcome by a few. The ones who would only say "those damn tourists…", not realizing the livelihood of the town depended on those "damn tourists" throughout the very short season of the year when they would come in. The Porch in the Ghost Town was where most would be, drinking beer and playing music, watching those tourists come in and out of the gift shop while also having dinner at the Starlight, which opened at five o'clock. Not much else to do. The joke I heard early on said that Highway 118, a gravel road for many years, had been paved for the beer trucks.

Some aspects changed. Having a camp to come back to when needed or wanting to became a plus, but something was off. I started developing roots. Not what I set out to accomplish almost a year ago. An odd feeling I needed to overcome. Ever slowly, the enjoyment of being at The Oasis took care of it. The days went by, so did the weeks and the few months of winter. The depth of this magical space materialized with much healing coming my way and Spirit in love with his new found freedom from day one, running around like a kid on a newly acquired playground while keeping his eyes on me in his usual constant manner. A friend of mine from Houston dropped off some pecan wood already cut and split. The result of his tree orchard devastated by a recent hurricane. He came to Big Bend with his motorcycle on the bed of his truck while trailering the wood. I dug three fire pits next to each other, large logs were placed all around, and appeared a wonderful cooking area which could seat a dozen people. I started calling it the Center of my Universe, all surrounded by designs made with local rocks. I decided it would be Lance's resting place. Today, opposite of him, it is also my Mother's. One fire pit to produce coals with a tripod and chain hanging over it for stews, one for a Dutch Oven, the last one topped by a grate for grilling. Life off the grid I kept thinking, this is how it should be done. Back to the basics. It did not take long to acquire a 40 foot shipping container to store items, which to this day I have no clue how they got here. A local resident, stopping by one day, gave me the idea to tilt the container, attach a 40 foot gutter to the edge of the roof, and with the loan of a 300 gallon water tank from my friends and neighbors up the road, I would have rain water. Drinking water came from Terlingua. A couple solar panels kept my electronics and lights running. The greatest local telephone and Internet company installed a phone line with DSL, and before I knew it, we were Home. It took me a long time to mentally call this "Home". Deep down I only wanted to be on the road, but where else could we go in winter time and duplicate such a space?

Big Bend National Park. The least visited park in this country at arms reach and we spent many nights under its stars. 800,000 acres, a Chihuahuan desert sharing 118 miles with Mexico, the Rio Grande River being its natural border. Big Bend State Park, another 300,000 acres of playground. Terlingua Ranch on which The Oasis is located, another close to one million acres with hundreds of miles of unpaved roads. No lack of places to go and experience. Little towns around us all within reach. Alpine, about 55 miles away, Marfa, Ft Davis, Marathon, all around 100 miles. Presidio reached by riding River Road, another one of the country's most beautiful road, and if we wanted to, we could easily cross into Mexico. I would not have a problem spending most of our winters here. For now.

We fell into what is called "Terlingua time". Meaning the mental and physical disregard towards a clock or a calendar. An easy lifestyle when days would pass by without leaving The Oasis. To my surprise. My Mother would even ask me, "So what did you do all day?" I never knew the answer only knowing we lived the moments as they came. We were in the "now" as never before, and all of this because of a piece of land purchased in the middle of nowhere. I was not being lazy, Spirit either, with always something to do, it just took longer to do it. Whatever it might be. Taking photos, reading, cooking, sleeping, playing, hiking, riding new roads, transferring water, writing our journal, arranging the shipping container and mostly thinking, all with very few visitors. Hardly, besides the UPS truck, any vehicles came by. Why would anyone want to? There came days I forced ourselves towards a chosen destination. I knew we would not see those three million acres in one winter, there was no rush to go anywhere. Odd as it may seem, partly due no doubt to my gypsy blood running in profusion, I at the same time looked forward to the beginning of Spring to head on back up north, as the heat of Big Bend could reach into the upper 120's. I might have been slightly confused as being gladly rooted against my will for these few months of the year.

The weather so perfect throughout the coming months. As the year before it froze some nights. In the mornings a ritual started taking place as we would play frisbee with the ice forming in Spirit's water bowl. It even snowed a couple days. By noon, mostly short sleeve T-shirt time. The most gorgeous sunrises and sunsets never stopped. It became a daily occurrence and that is when I found out the dynamics changed when suddenly a camera stood between us. Without photos, the scenes are the ones I remember the best. It became an evening show, front row seat always facing west with nothing in between us and the horizon, Spirit being so content. Some days, the local adventures awaited. River Road to Presidio with its great bakery became my favorite. We would come back with bags of Mexican pastries and bread purchased while warm out of the oven. Highway 170 from Terlingua is 66 miles long. Sometimes winding, some straight stretches, up and down the hills, always following the Rio Grande. I started calling it the "Road of a Thousand Pictures". One could walk it and take a photo with every step. How many roads are there when one could ride along constantly looking at another country? This is when I came to the conclusion we had gone too fast this first year now closing in on us. Up north or on the way down, all the treasures passed by so quickly not savored, including spending a month in Halfway and its vicinity. The quality of the moments surfacing versus the volume of destinations in sight. I started noticing riders doing what we used to do. The big loop, as it is called here. From Alpine to Terlingua, into the Park to Boquillas, back to Terlingua, on to Presidio, up to Marfa and back to Alpine. All in one day with the bragging rights they had seen it all. Ridden it, yes, seen it all, no.

Often drawn to Big Bend National Park, crossing its gate always brought on an extra wave of peace descending upon me. One of my favorite spots is Sotol Look Out, from where 13 miles as the crow flies, one can see Santa Helena Canyon and Mexico. The greatest sunsets took place right where we stood for many nights. A couple of them left me speechless as the sun went into hiding with its unimaginable colors so delicately painted, at the same time a couple storms could be seen on the horizon with their rain diagonally bouncing off the valley. A giant stage of many square miles and no one rarely ever around. More amazement. We were somehow being transported to the right place at the right time.

October 13th, Lance's 30th birthday came and went. What a day. Acceptance was so difficult as it is to this very moment. We spent the day at The Oasis, and when evening came, I lit candles all around my Center of the Universe staying up all night trying to find him throughout the stars above me. This is what I wrote at the time:

"The Stars were bright last night as I looked up into the
darkness of the night without a moon and searched for you.
I know you were there watching as you have done since you

left us. I am so sorry that I get angry lately because you are not here. I miss you so much and there are no words strong enough that will express it. This journey has always been dedicated to you, but today, this day, it is tougher and harder than the others. I so much wish you were here. My flesh and blood. How can this be? The storm has passed you know, but the swells remain. Thirty years today. You are 30 years old. I will not get to hug you this time around, mess up your hair, sing for you, watch you eat your favorite cake, tease you some more. How can there be joy when only tears roll down this face unable to smile today. There is a lump in my throat. I cannot swallow my emotions. The questions have still been left behind unanswered and the wall has only grown taller and higher. I cannot even see the other side anymore as much as I try. I have taken a beautiful path lately Lance. I know it because I write about it and the pictures are here to prove it. You tell me so. You wanted me to, "it's all good" were your last words, yet my own thoughts keep slamming down on this unfinished and rough cement bottom. I sometimes just don't know anymore, my despair becomes overwhelming and the more time passes by, the more I am left standing here all alone, missing your presence and the aura radiated by you just being. Fair, unfair, unjust, who knows anymore as I truly don't. I am only left numb to endure the injustice which made you so suffer, especially on your last day. What faith changed this beautiful young man that you are in the pictures that I don't want to forget and only remember you as such? I want to scream out loud, bring you back, and at the same time, I bow under the weight of this life that has added this giant black hole I feel sinking in deeper and deeper. My journey is my savior, my journal is my soundboard. Comments and e-mails from strangers and friends extending kindly their own emotions towards us are my portals to the world, to the bit of sunshine that tries to warm me up daily. Mother Nature's space is the only stage I know how to walk on anymore. How lucky can I be that she has embraced me so tightly to make some of my days more tolerable than others. Spirit has become my faithful companion. We take care of each other. Beat up and almost stripped down himself of his own soul not too long ago from much abuse, we both stand together trying to cope with it all the best we can. He is all I have, I am all he has. We are alike and so often lean on each other for the support needed to keep us going. Why did it all go wrong when all was so right? Why did my boy not even see the hope of his first 30 years? And still, with twice those years on my shoulders, here I stand. I cannot give up. Could I? That would be too easy. Right? The seasons and lessons will go on, as I will as long as I am allowed to. The leaves will turn brown and gold, they will drop and reappear yearly as also your birthday and the anniversary of your departure will. I can only hope that I am planted deep and strongly enough to not get uprooted some day by too much emotions. At the same time, I know now I am not the only one wearing this coat of such sorrow. I thought I was for a long time. The reality is not so, as it seems every family has suffered such a loss of a loved one. I cannot be the bad example and quit my tracks. My thoughts are also with you who are on this same path. Words from others coming in have meant a lot to me, they are that bridge toward this island of spiritual comfort. Happy Birthday Lance, with the wish that those green eyes of yours are full of the new life you have embraced. I miss you, I miss you so much."

I learned to be more confrontational towards life. Friendship with my Mother reached new heights, astounded how right she could be on so many aspects of this present. While falling into the wonders of my surroundings, I plunged into the true meaning and rightness of her own words. "Life was not meant to be easy, you have been given the hardest test there is, but you have to make it and pull through". The discoveries, mental and physical, all adding up. New pathways around us coming our direction.

Riding Indian Head Trail, the rocks reminded me of sculptures taking on so many different shapes I started naming them. Old Maverick Road, 12 miles of unpaved sometimes easy, sometimes not, much depending on past weather, leading to Santa Helena Canyon where we would try to arrive before sunrise for its sublime show. We always stopped at "Luna's Jacal". A dwelling half under ground, its back wall a huge rock fallen off the mountain. Gilberto Luna lived there until 1947. He passed away at the ripe age of 108, leaving behind 54 children. I thought it would have been interesting to chat with him around a campfire. What stories I am sure he must have had. A couple miles off Old Maverick Road, on a road a bit bumpier, we often went to Terlingua Abaja, not too far from the Rio Grande River. It used to be a farming village which supplied the miners and the ranchers of the area from 1900 to the 1930's. So much history before all was overgrazed and turned into a park. Sometimes we could cross the Rio Grande by foot when the water's low enough. There is a hike made out of stairs on the other side. Rafting appeared out of the question as they did not allow dogs on the river, all with permits, mainly through the few rafting companies in Terlingua. Having dinner one night in town, I sat next to a river guide and curious me, I asked him "How was it?" He turned around as I heard him say "Do you want the short version or the long version?" I replied I would be happy with the short version. "It is just a bunch of rocks and some water" he said, seriously. I guessed by then, he only did it for the money. Another day at the office.

Day of the Dead is celebrated every November in Terlingua. Viva la Historia which took place on the same weekend in the Ghost Town, was a once in a lifetime experience to attend. A privilege, an event filled with emotions, colors, music, much food and best of all, many stories. The town invited the past residents who used to work the mines, along with everyone born in and around the Chisos during those times. An incredible task as hundreds showed up, an event covered by the New York Daily News, as well as Dallas and Houston newspapers. Not a "reality show", it was reality. We were among families who returned bringing with them their children, cousins, aunts, uncles and friends. We sat with them around the many tables which had been set up for the occasion and ate the food so abundant while mainly listening to their past with much respect and admiration. Summers were not easy in the Ghost Town, especially for those working the mines. I was a passerby welcomed with open arms as if being part of this emotional event. My intend had been to stay back and only try to overhear some of the stories, maybe taste some of the food if offered, but not to be invited and sitting with them creating an instant friendship unlike ever experienced. A bonfire in the evening and the next day more music, more food and much dancing. Tools were provided to clean up the cemetery and everyone, including myself, dug in. It was then the Day of the Dead and candles were lit on every tomb. Memorabilia appeared to celebrate the departed. A bottle of wine, a few cans of beer, some loose change, photos of the departed, trinkets, some chips and salsa. All filling the soul as I had never experienced such times, never understanding why and how in this fashion the dead can be memorialized. They were, myself glad to be part of it by celebrating Lance in a fashion unknown to me before.

There is still present, a platform on which part of me floats through life. A path of thoughts with only smiles stamped on by footprints from others. I call it the "good channel". Filled by characteristics of a recent past life that obviously left its mark, I always feel so fortunate when it emerges during the least expected times of need. It is the part of me that enjoys approaching others, total strangers, and engaging in conversations. Ones which make me feel afterwards appreciative towards the time they give me. I always felt the same facing Mother Nature or attending events as above. I loved open arms as mine were also.

One morning, I found my laptop moved and the batteries were down, so I naturally wondered happened. As I booted it, I noticed a new page in the journal. It looked like Spirit stayed up all night adding a bit of his own thoughts.

"It has been cold tonight, I am wondering when he is going to get my coats out. My hair is so short, especially under my neck and belly, that only my shivering gives him a hint of covering me. I don't like to lay down right in front of the heater because it dries up my nose, the sunburn I get while riding is bad enough. I do need to thank him for the sunscreen at times, and also for removing that stupid wind-shield on which I kept bumping my head and was blocking all the good oncoming smells. So yes, I love to ride, feel the wind, the faster the better and the scents are like being in Heaven. They sometimes pass by too quickly, not letting me savor them. I have my own Ural sidecar, wish it was a BMW like his, but, Oh well! it does have a BMW emblem on it. I fake it. My buddies who see me at least think so. They have to walk, I ride. I am not a mean dog, but it is my job to protect this rig of ours. Sometimes he is happy when I growl, even bark, sometimes he tells me to quit. I have a hard time distinguishing when I should and when I should not. So I do it to be on the safe side. Humans can be funny about this kind of behavior. I often feel they don't know what they want. We have spent weeks in desolate areas, and he sure has been happy when I warn him minutes ahead about anyone nearing the campsite. He has such poor hearing. I do have the good life. He has never trained me, so I took it upon myself to let him be and just live his life as I live my *own, especially when he is tapping this keyboard with his fingers and too often talking to it. So strange. No sense disturbing the flow. I would probably just be told to do this or that. As long as I get my food twice a day and even better now, as I fooled him that I would not eat dry food. He does not. Why should I? I know what he eats, I have tried it a couple times without a happy ending getting sick from both ends. He was not very happy either. That might be why we have a new tent now. I am so glad being a dog. I don't think I could stand his life. Cooking, having to be in control of the motorcycle, thinking too much, all too busy for me. I live a simple life, I don't have laundry to do, I clean myself a bit every day just so the dreaded baths are not as often. The only thing I had to teach him, and I think he finally got it, is to relax when we are out, especially in the deserts and forests. There is so much to listen to and so many smells that I need to stop and concentrate a bit harder. He does too now, we are finally in tune with each other. No complaints. I even have my nails done weekly. He only once clipped a bit too short. I forgave him. I have my own electric blanket when we ride, many pairs of sunglasses, a cool helmet with all kinds of stickers on it. I just wish he would get me some clear lenses for those goggles. Does he really think I can see through them at night? Yes, humans are so strange. So I give a little. He gets into his kicks taking pictures of me standing by a ledge or on a rock. He is really slow taking them and does not like me to move. So I wait, wait, roll my eyes, but he wants me to look at him. Sometimes he even says "treat... treat...", knowing too well the treats are in the trunk of the sidecar! I just wish I could see all the pictures because he forgets that also too often. The worst is when we stop for fuel or at a pull out, for that matter anywhere with people around. It's like they have never seen a dog in a sidecar with goggles and a helmet on, and they have to take my picture. They even become demanding calling out loud "Look here doggy... look here...". When are they going to understand I am not a doggy, but a dog. When all done, I don't get anything from them, not even the resemblance of a treat. I like it when he leaves me in the sidecar and walks away, as then, I start growling at the people and scare them. Now, that is much fun. I hope we stay on the road for a long time and do much more riding, as long as I am not too hot or too cold. I know that my life is much better than my buddies who stayed back at the shelter in Georgia. I still have night-mares about my previous life, but at least now I get many hugs a day, my butt scratched and much love. I knew my hours were counted before he rescued me and I will always be thankful to him about that. He is a great buddy to have and I know he also thinks the same of me."*

The months went by. How fascinating having been on the road for over a year. We continued exploring this vast neighborhood. The Old Marathon Road loop with deep sand and my heart often skipping a beat. Pinto Canyon Road steeply dropping at times, located further east from Marfa to Presidio, more local roads on Terlingua Ranch around us. We attended Art Walk in Alpine, Chinati Days in Marfa, camped in Chinati Hot Springs a few days and more events in Terlingua. We experienced a Powwow, a personal tour of the Hobby-Eberly telescope a bit North of Fort Davis and entertained children in their school in Valentine. The destinations never dried out.

Blankets of frost on some January mornings. A quiet Christmas, the same with New Year's Eve and Day. Nothing changed here in the desert. It did not recognize the dates or probably forgot about them. The Oasis brought on the memories of past years when the common denominator of happy and good times filled with love was family. We had shrunk but the heart reopened filled with warmth. A huge present came my way through one of the many phone calls with my Mother. She decided to come to the States for at least a month and in addition wanted me to have a dwelling of some sort at The Oasis. Time to change gears, get organized and use a calendar for her good news. We were to meet in Atlanta, 1,200 miles or so away and spend three weeks on the Georgia coast. It became my responsibility to find us accommodations in quiet surroundings and dog friendly. Excited, the phone calls became daily going over the details and the reservations needed. It came time to pack up and head back east for the many miles waiting. Tidy it all up here, hold the mail, let my few friends and neighbors know we were leaving.

Bags and all, we allowed ourselves much time to get there without rushing. Slowly putting on the miles, I wanted to fully experience, as learned, this new old leg of our journey. That day arrived as we took Highway 95 for the first stop in Del Rio where we camped by the Amistad Reservoir and spent a day visiting the Whitehead Museum. The next one, in Acuna, Mexico, mainly eating real Mexican fare. I love outdoor vendors and eating while standing up having spent my whole life working in kitchens with never much time to sit down. We played the tourists. We should have gone through San Antonio after leaving Del Rio, but I wanted to avoid the mainstream and we had time. We dropped to Eagle Pass, and after a few hours of searching I could not find a campsite. I did not care for the town which seemed a bit sleazy and uncomfortable. No choice but a motel as much as I never liked them. They gave me a feeling of loneliness cooped up between four walls emphasized by a television screen staring at me which I never watched, and always wondering how clean the sheets were. Who had slept in the bed? My sleeping bag would do much better laid out on top or on the floor over my pad. We again crossed a bridge into Mexico for the day, Piedras Negras. Even though early, I could already smell the street food being prepared. I noticed, how could I not, every store keeper washing their sidewalk space with buckets filled with soap and water, then swept with a broom. Nice touch to keep the dust down for a while. It gave me a good feeling of care and pride from the local merchants. This little town differed from Acuna as the neighborhood slowly came to life. More street shops opening up, a big square of vendors, ponchos, pinatas, hats, boots and so much more for sale. Still the only ones walking around, the merchants were already trying to lighten my wallet. Little tacos satisfied my hunger, tasty little things, a fresh banana milk drink, more window shopping and time to cross the bridge back to Eagle Pass.

That is when the route became confusing. We were distancing ourselves from Atlanta, not getting any closer, time left getting shorter as the days were numbered, a new concept for me. After one look at the map I concluded we were too far south, as much as I would have liked to continue in that direction. We did not need to turn around, only change our direction towards San Antonio, which we passed through followed by a couple nights of camping in Luling. No lost time, yet I knew I was dragging. San Antonio brought back memories from the year before as we backtracked to its downtown after setting up camp. Having never seen the Alamo, there it was to my surprise, right in the middle of downtown, a Fort much smaller than imagined. The urban maze welcomed us while parking surrounded with shady characters roaming around. Never being one to lock the bike, put our SPOT, GPS and everything else away, the space lacked a comfort zone. The fact that no photos were allowed to be taken inside the Alamo made it easy. I did not go in. Spirit and I just stood there for a while watching the crowds passing by, carriages filled with tourists, more of them as we took a few steps on the crowded River Walk. I knew we were going to have a hard time with the upcoming big cities, but the prize of spending much quality time with my Mother could only be a good compromise. Before we left Luling, the highlight ended up being The City Market, where to this day I have never tasted such incredible BBQ. Mentioned by a friend of a friend; that is how the word gets around. No plates, all served on brown paper and no utensils either. A swinging door as one entered from the dining room to place the order and pick it up while exiting through another. A dark room with the smoker against a wall blackened from the years, a huge butcher block worn out in the center from the cuts of many knives, four men of impressive size standing around with caps on, a thermometer stuck into a brisket, all immobile as if in the middle of brain surgery. I did not dare disturb them and waited to be asked for my order. BBQ in the State of Texas is serious business. I knew I almost pushed my luck when in a low tone I asked if I could take a photo. I did after he replied "You can when I have my back turned".

We rode Highway 90 avoiding busy Highway 10, which at some point we would have to. From then on, we faced the traffic of Houston, Beaumont, Lafayette, Baton Rouge, avoided New Orleans as much as its food attracted me, Mobile and Montgomery, as by then the state of Alabama welcomed us. We made good time and stayed on a schedule given myself with no choice in the matter. The familiar city of Atlanta appeared on the horizon. My heart sank remembering how and why we left the area not so long ago. Having arranged for us to stay in the yard of a friend's construction business, it turned out to be a good choice for the couple nights awaiting my Mother's arrival. I took care of the logistics. With a hotel room already booked I rented a car. My Mother, at 81, was not going to ride with Spirit. I stored Old Faithful and moved our bags, the ones we would need for the coming month, and before I knew it, I drove! I found myself a bit off within the lanes, quite rusty from not being behind a steering wheel, Spirit and I more than ever paying attention amidst the continuous flow of traffic. From the deserted roads of The Oasis to now, a culture shock. The highlight driving to the airport arrived. Georgia had always been one of the most hospitable states, yet, the roads were not. It seemed the cars turned into lethal weapons compounded by the fact almost everyone on their cell phone, some I noticed with paperwork on their lap. Not as bad as putting on mascara while texting, eating a cheeseburger and yelling at the kids in the backseat, I heard this happened. Swaying to the left, to the right, cutting us off, as once in their cars, the hospitality factor disappeared, the drivers reinforced with all the powers for an assault "winner takes all" on the roads. Maybe too much NASCAR watching.

What a glorious moment seeing my Mother coming up the escalator towards the waiting area. Still beautiful, petite as always and colorfully dressed. She looked and felt great. Big long hugs, a step back, more hugs, kisses, checking each other out, big smiles, both choked up a little, maybe much. A reunion of warmth and love. She managed to pick up her suitcase with my back turned, but I grabbed it from her right away. She felt good and happy. We were free to move on towards the car with Spirit waiting, luckily with cool weather. This being the first time meeting him, he had a nice welcome for her, maybe not to the degree I expected, but he was not in his normal environment. I knew as time settled down they would become better friends. We drove on to the hotel for one night, downtown by Lenox Square.

The day we went to Tybee Island happened to be Lance's fourth year passing away anniversary. I did not have to be alone, the 300 mile drive filled with conversations of our memories, much laughter, tears, rainbows of emotions. She possessed better than me the ability to bring back happy moments, funny ones, the jokes Lance would always go on repeating with his dry sense of humor, no doubt taken after me. He would always make everyone laugh without himself cracking a smile reaching into their soul all at the same time. We did not solve the why's and how's, but gratified by sitting together with her ability to relate. Maybe the older generation is stronger having endured a harsher life than us and witnessed so many more tragedies. Maybe their acceptance is more present, a precious commodity in life.

We settled into a nice motel on the beach pretty quickly, a beach where unfortunately as I found out later, dogs were not allowed. Kind, my Mother asked if we wanted to move on to another town. It would be alright, I did not want to get back on the road again and we were going to sight-see many other beaches which allowed dogs. As good as she felt, she was always ready to come back within a few hours. She was 81 after all. At 60, I myself often ready towards the end of the day to return and relax in her company. Such luxurious times. We ate breakfast and a big late lunch out every day and a light snack in the room for dinner. I did not cook for a month. We followed our noses and sometimes smells throughout the streets as we walked in search for good meals and endless conversations, the scenarios of her moving to the States included. Deep down, I knew she would never really move, but I never stopped trying to embellish my arguments and pleading. She did not drive anymore, where would she move when so comfortable in Munich. Grocery stores within minutes, a few nice restaurants, great public transportation, healthcare and a few good friends. Of course the move would allow us to be closer. No other reason. She was so attached to her furniture, the beautiful little knick knacks throughout her third floor two bedroom apartment, her paintings and photos from all over the world when she extensively traveled. What could I say? I knew it would be hard to undertake such a move as much as she agreed with me and wanted to.

Tybee Island turned out to be a good choice for us. Quiet, barely any traffic and a beautiful boardwalk. Since we could not be on the beach with Spirit, that is where we mostly walked. We checked out the light-house, Savannah a couple times and its historical district, more eating, window shopping, much more talking. One day, we decided to visit St. Simon Island south of us. A big mistake. The road could not follow the ocean because of the many marshes compounded with two narrow lanes jammed with traffic. We quickly found this was where everyone else took roots. Lost a couple times, we arrived in town while following miles of traffic and going around the blocks searching for parking. A space with a meter we fed a bag full of quarters into, I must add. The town seemed to be going through some growing pains and yet, the stores did not open until five o'clock in the afternoon. I imagined the scene while in season. It must have been a horrific time. At one point, my Mother only wanted to sit in the car. Spirit and I went to the lighthouse for a brief time to take a couple photos. When we came back, she and I looked at each other and understood without a word, grand time to return to our little quiet Island.

It did not matter much after that day where we went. Mostly resting, going nowhere with a quality of time spent together mattering to the both of us not having much of it left as all flew by so quickly. I started to feel the pain of the future separation so close in sight. It was not always as such between us. Our disagreements used to be much stronger, hard headed. There was, existing in years past, much dislike towards each other's thoughts. With much understanding a new born friendship started to take place and opened up the stage for many conversations with no boundaries. I don't know why it takes so long in one's life to realize such matters, to understand the priorities present and accept each other for who we are, as so much in the big picture does not really matter. She slowly came around accepting my lifestyle, understanding the healing journey both Spirit and I were on. Having never been on the internet before, we went through the countless photos of the many spaces Spirit and I visited. She stopped asking me if I ever thought about ending this path and getting back to my profession as a chef. She knew of my pain deep inside and of my inner conscience which never ceased battling the invisible opponents, the resonance of the battlefields never diminishing. She understood I worked hard on extinguishing those sounds, as well as the feels and the images which went along with them. I was learning to live in this new arena with its highs and lows, seeking help through some kind of makeshift morality which many overlooked too often. Mother Nature's beauty, as she never held back her offerings when together in her company. Like my Mother, she also held me up when down, never putting away a palette that could only be her's and no one else's. Our life was a tunnel we traveled through seeking for windows so sporadically found. Those see through panes were the incoming rewards, the photos taken, all were the energy much needed to go on as their shutters always wide open, never filtering their brightness and vision.

Back in Atlanta, with a big void as my Mother's plane was now flying over the Atlantic. The good byes and hugs lasted forever. Unanswered were so many questions regarding her moving, myself seeing everything in a much more simple manner. Sell your belongings, move, rent a new apartment, buy whatever is necessary, and you are done. It does not work as such when up in age, often at any age. Being more tired than she led me to believe, I did not even know if she would ever come back as the flight wore her down. It all added to the feelings hovering over me that first night back in the big city. I knew I would be the one having to go at times and leave Spirit behind with some trustworthy friends. One step at the time. Unfortunately such steps regarding her and me did not yet have a direction.

I pulled my map out. Back to ground zero our next destination was Moab and its vicinity. Utah. A state I have never ceased to explore. Some familiar spaces, others inviting heard from friends. We stopped in Birmingham and spent a couple days at the Barber Museum. An incredible motorcycle museum, where the founder, Mr. Barber, took us around in areas normally closed to the public. A slight detour, spending a couple nights in Memphis to visit Elvis's house, a tour more commercial than ever imagined. Another couple nights in Lubbock while back in Texas, with a brief visit to the Buddy Holly and the Wind Mill Museums. Feeling rushed and obsessed with getting to Moab, I was already imagining the red rocks everywhere, some maybe covered with snow, the trails I had seen on the map, a center for the outdoors.

I would soon run out of adjectives describing Moab, all of Utah for that matter. One can try to not be repetitious, but the language itself contains only so many words expressing the feeling of being overwhelmed. I had a hard time keeping my eyes on the road while Spirit, as usual, kept turning his head towards me just about every eight seconds reminding me to pay attention being at the helm. One of my first thoughts was, as when arriving at the Grand Canyon, Zion or Big Bend National Park, "What happened here?" Staring with every mile passing by, some major construction which had taken place over millions of years. The giant cliffs, of all reds perhaps from overcoming the struggles they were portraying, rocks balancing with no means of support, shapes of all forms and their shadows slowly moving on, all so perfectly engineered by the past waters flowing, the winds traveling as giant sandblasters, heat and ice. All chiseled from what was an ocean floor to today's massive canyons and formations. We found ourselves camping on the Colorado River, and there was an incredible excitement to begin the first ride. Fuel check, oil check, Spirit securely harnessed, water and provisions, nuts and bolts checked, SPOT, cameras. The usual drill. I did not bypass any detail as I never did for every morning we rolled. Where to go? How about starting from the beginning? What beginning? Calming down. We could stay as long as we wanted always forgetting that notion. It takes time to shed the past programming from a life lived with a clock.

Arches National Park. Why not? This is where everyone started as we followed, waiting for the day to emerge when such would stop and we'd be the finders of the gems of Nature unknown to others. We entered its space and the vastness of the land ahead of us slowed me down. We will not leave any stones unturned! Every step to be savored, every color and shape digging so deep into my sights having never been among such an unimaginable array. We camped on BLM land before the banks of the Colorado River were purposely burnt down and campgrounds erected. When the past free red welcoming soil turned into cans of sardines, a too familiar scene I would see in the future when returning and avoiding. BLM managed 1.8 million acres. They eventually picked the most scenic spaces for campers to avoid them being isolated and truly taking in the surroundings. Night and day had its own weather. By noon, short sleeve T-shirt, as the sun dropped behind the rocks, the electric heated riding gear and coat for Spirit came out. I did not witness many cold sunrises, never having the heart to get Spirit out of his own sleeping bag. That was my excuse anyway.

Hardly containing myself, we barely touched on The Arches wanting a taste of everywhere. The other parks with many entrances in contrasting regions were cut off by different canyons. Off Highway 191 north, we made a left on Highway 313 and entered the Islands in the Skies. Canyonland. The roads were smooth and curvy with many pull outs for my camera and a break for Spirit. I found more free BLM camping above 5,000 feet, and even though it warmed up, 22 degrees at six a.m. instead of 20, a move would have to wait. For a couple miles, the road with guard rails on each side was called The Neck, the only tip which had not been subjected to erosion. The views went on for more than a hundred miles. We sat there for a long time looking at Shafer Trail and its switchbacks, all a bit intimidating along with a desire to ride it uphill. On that day the trail remained closed, and as imagined while on our ride to the area, patches of snow were present in deep contrast with the red rocks. The Colorado River deep below us, the White Rim Trail above it so mysteriously following its edges. What a scenario. Further away, we could barely see the Maze and the Needles. All a work of art.

We ate lunch on that same overlook due to a routine started while near Moab. City Market and its parking lot became our social gathering every morning before or after food shopping, sometimes both times. This is where everyone came for provisions, and why stock up when we could shop almost daily. Of course, Spirit as always the main attraction and I did not mind the continuous chatting with others who shared the same enthusiasm for the outdoors and the area. I learned a lot through those conversations. Mainly where to go and not to go. We were not four wheel drive and limited in our whereabouts compared to some of those incredible off road vehicles. So when lunchtime arrived, we laid down a little blanket and took out the three cheese Artisan bread, some Kalamato olives of all different colors and tastes, some marinated mushrooms and roasted garlic, all with much water. Spirit ate some bread, that is the extend of his human food consumption. I could not have him stare at me the whole time. Coming out of past weeks in an urban setting, I found him so much more alive and truly living. He loved growling when in his sidecar and myself a bit far. I could always hear him and listen afterward to the comments of the ones that passed by him "Great security you have there...".

Thirteen hours of sleep one night. Spirit never woke me up. It surprised me, even more, him not calling the animal abuse center! Others often asked why we did not ride every day. We lived on the road and dipped into a quality of time unlike the past year. As an emphasis to such moments, it happened right in the Moab area. It could have been the vastness which made me realize we would come back, as we did a few times during the coming years. We would because we had to savor every mile passing by, even the same miles when the weather changed and the hues took on some glows unlike the times before. It was endless while being served a richness of life which did not revolve around the wealth of a hard currency, but in the hearts and relationships with others upon a stage with a privilege to pass through.

We moved on a few miles further north. Not up the mountain, not yet. More free camping. I could not have it any other way. Nice and quiet, a dirt road to nowhere and we were off it by maybe a couple hundred yards. As always, I had the biggest feeling of satisfaction when finding a good spot knowing we could stay for a while without being disturbed. I switched Old Faithful's rear tire to a knobby one and we went on to assault Potash Road and Shafer Trail. What a day to remember. Took some air out of the tires for better grip, double checked everything related to our safety, hunger, thirst, and off we went. I made our first video with a camera mounted behind Spirit. We rode to Dead Horse Point a couple days earlier and looked down. Now below it, we looked up. The road narrowed at some point where we stopped. Above me, a couple thousand feet up, were the look outs; below me, 1,200 feet or so, ran the Colorado River. Millions of years of erosion and us right in the middle of it, a humbling experience. A doable road, the rear wheel did spin a few times, we took all day. So many other places I wanted to stop and take photos, they were not too safe to do such. I later found out the road was used by trucks in the 1940's for the ore and uranium miners. I felt a bit silly learning if trucks made it in the past, there should have not been any reservation on my part to make the run. Soft sand at times, most of it blown away by the winds leaving flat layers of slick rocks with sharp edges resembling shelves and steps, all mixed in with scattered softball size rocks. Nothing too challenging, only demanding caution.

Those days led to more riding, unfortunately a bit over my head. Too much confidence, not the right vehicle for the roads taken which were technically impassable for Old Faithful. It also led to a new lesson and a word which I afterwards often expressed out of need and not desire "U-turn". I should have never considered going up Chicken Corners through Hurray Pass. All with again shelf-like ledges, but taller and sharper, hairpin turns I could not right off negotiate, and a deep water crossing which put an end to the rides for a while, the level being too high. We did cross it while Spirit's car filled up to the brim like a bath tub, made it to the crest of the last hill, and the engine died. A first for us. The end of our present time in Moab. We arranged to be towed to Salt Lake City for some costly repairs.

After being towed two hundred and thirty miles, Old Faithful was dropped off at a good old-fashioned independent BMW motorcycle shop. The sensor submerged had gone bad and surprised the mechanic, as being the original, should have never lasted 181,000 miles. A new one already in the mail arrived quickly. On the Internet, a very useful tool, it only took minutes to find one. We stayed with some new friends, enjoying their hospitality and good food. Three days later, the repair completed, we were ready to roll. Where else to go but back to Moab. We were not done, we will never be done with Utah. Dark from the black clouds in the skies, I could see the rain and smell it all around us. The roads were slick and yet not a drop touched us. All along, smooth hills were in our company while approaching Moab. We climbed up Highway 6, and when dropping from Soldier Pass at 7,400 feet, the sun broke through the clouds and the familiar red rocks appeared so comforting. A calmness invaded me as we approached the dirt road we had just left a few days ago and found it unoccupied. I did not like breaking down, but I looked at the big picture. Friends helping out, strangers lending a hand and us returning to the path we were on. We went back to The Arches. We re-entered the park a few times each visit as a new one, impossible to see it all.

A few days later, the starter howled with every turn of the key and needed to be replaced. Durango had a shop which we called and ordered a rebuilt one. A good deal since we could also camp in their backyard. The breakdowns were starting to add up. I figured with such repairs it would be a long time before the same parts broke again. The plus side. The wallet getting shallow, the minus side. We said our good byes to Moab and new friends which we saw one more time and on towards east the wheels rolled. The starter waited, a repair I could have easily done myself which I learned for the next time.

As we left, we encountered some of the worst riding days since being on the road. I wished so much we stayed in Durango one more day after the repair, a true reminder to keep up with the weather forecast. Hesitating through a snow storm, we pushed on beyond Cortez. A foolish act. I thought I had slowed down, but southern Utah emerged on the tip of my tongue. The snow went away, replaced by formidable winds and large size hail, the icing on the cake. No pun intended. They hurt on a moving motorcycle, like bullets shot down from above and then changing direction to hit from the front. Spirit most likely wished having his windshield back, yet he learned to dive down into the nose of his sidecar and take shelter. Smart. We did not talk for quite a while. Our destinations were Bluff, Valley of the Gods, Mexican Hat, Monument Valley, and more, away from this unusual wintery Colorado weather. Those infamous spaces by the San Juan River I heard so much about, seen so many photos. Of course we made it. Both exhausted, my hands and arms sore from fighting with a handlebar which wanted to always turn the opposite way, Spirit shivering even with his coat and heated blanket on which by then were both soaked. A campground sign a couple miles west of Bluff turned out to be the biggest relief ever. A BLM campground with a fee even though with no power and water. It did not matter at the time, shelter being the only word on my mind. Without any amenities it probably would be pretty quiet and empty from the majority of campers wanting all the creature comforts while outdoors. If that made any sense! The safety of dispersed camping was in reality changing. Unfortunately, a reality present more so today. The numbers of homeless were growing steadily, amazingly, they were also the ones with drug and alcohol addictions in search of items they could steal and sell, the scenario found around Sedona spreading. Those thoughts in years past would have never crossed my mind as they were nonexistent. Or so I thought. I felt safer when I saw other campers, even if a quarter or half a mile away. It became a habit going over and introducing ourselves while chatting about such safety in the wilderness and realizing not being the only one thinking as such. As we did not ride every day, and some also stayed at camp at times enjoying the daylight hours, we always agreed on watching each other's back. It did happen a few times when an odd car would drive by us and stop at the next campsite with the tenants gone. We would immediately ride towards them and of course they would take off. I knew they were not around to take photos.

Population 360, our kind of town, Bluff reminded me of Terlingua with all the locals knowing each other. One gas station, a couple restaurants and one grocery store 45 miles away near Monument Valley. Constantly changing weather. An aspect of the journey we could always count on. As we regrouped, the skies again turned blue, the temperatures became tolerable, summer seemed to be right around the corner. Time to discover Valley of the Gods. I don't know if because of its name, the photos seen or just an intuition, I strongly sensed as it does to this day, a strong pull towards it. Valley of the Gods has to be one of my favorite spaces to spend a few weeks and live it up. A well maintained 17 mile unpaved loop, sandstone buttes standing above us 1,200 feet at times, all sculptured by wind, ice and water having taken 250 million years to produce. The story goes, as Mother Earth mated with the Sun, the buttes are her soldiers standing tall protecting the land. From our first stay, I felt we were present by invitation only, and in future years, with much camping along the roads, there was always also a time to leave. We moved in within a couple days. I wanted to live on that land and feel its presence and everything else it contained. The names were many as I started reading the stories, myths maybe, but nothing wrong believing them.

Seven Sailors, sandstone monoliths and pinnacles with many geological features. Setting Hen Butte, and a bit further north a series of rock formations called Lime Ridge. A trapezoidal block of sandstone that looks like a hogan, the name for a traditional Navajo dwelling. In it are trapped children who were disobedient to the Sun Bearer and being punished. The story tells how the gods warned them not to steal animals, be respectful of people's property, but they repeatedly failed to follow their wishes. The Sun Bearer placed them in the hogan for four days trying to bring them to repentance. When this failed, the hogan turned into solid rock. They say when a person is near the site, they can hear the children crying. I did not find the hogan those days. Rooster Butte, Castle Butte, Balanced Rock, Lady in a Tub, Battleship Rocks, Devil's Window, Bell Butte, Scotsman Butte, many more given names. This home became much more than a stopover. A transformation took place as life again had slowed down. All so undisturbed with a larger than ever sense of peace, a detachment from our past while truly start-ing to have the ability to live more realistically in the "now". Dazzled, it became inexplicable and impossible for me at the time to put it all into words. The variety and brilliance of colors layered with silver brush and sundried desert greens, a geological masterpiece.

We took a ride through Monument Valley which left me tongue-tied. Yet the crowds, the touristic aspect of it all did not steer me to spend much time there. I decided we would come back another time, on a nicer day with much dancing of the clouds in the skies, some better times for photos. Its campground was a familiar scene crowded with many vehicles only inches apart. That stage took away the mystic feel of the territory laid out in front of us with the many larger sandstone buttes hardened by time.

Back in Valley of the Gods, sandstorms made their debut. I walked around with my full face helmet on, hopefully not scaring the spirits, while Spirit himself wearing his own helmet and goggles. We decided to move as it turned out not being fun when restricted in a tent. We needed to find a space without sand flying through the air, the winds themselves not bothering me much. Four miles or so away stood Gooseneck State Park. Packing and unpacking, a familiar routine. I had thought the river at the park as being only a bend where people went to look, not the surprise awaiting. Water flowing five miles while only progressing one linear mile. The finest example of an entrenched river. We arrived at a fairly large paved parking area with many cars and a couple buses. I quickly found an unpaved path veering to the left which took us towards some primitive sites. A bit further, the path narrowed increasingly and more campsites were present. I could not stop yet as by then seeing the point with a road barely present. We reached that point and looking back at the parking lot, the tourists were the size of ants. The winds blowing but with no sand, we were near a ledge that dropped about 1,000 feet to the river. Eerie. I set up quickly, and sheltered, we both laid down for the end of another day after being beaten up by the sandstorms. There were now only winds and I started wishing they would also go away. I remember dreaming about a barco lounger and a wide screen television, a kitchen with a refrigerator, an oven and even an ice maker. What a nightmare! As I woke up, only darkness surrounded me with a faint glow coming through the fabric of the tent. It was cold for this month of April, but the winds died down. I got out of the warm sleeping bag lined with an extra insert, put my pants and jacket over my thermal layers and went outside. I froze at the sight surrounding me. Not from the cold, but the indescribable background. The full moon appeared like a giant light bulb as the clouds were playing a game of shadows with the ledges and the flowing river. I knew it was not so, but I did tell myself "This is the best", as already witnessed so many "bests" and will continue to do so through the years. The "best" for that "now". Plain and simple. I stood for a while, a few steps to the right and a few to the left, finally pulling my chair out and sitting while shivering. It did not matter. Small price to pay feeling so privileged being there. As my eyelids became heavy I went back to the warm bag. I did not sleep well afterward. I dreamed of men in blue surrounding us, battling others wearing deer skins and having long black hair. I felt the air around me so disturbed from the images. In the morning, over a hot cup of coffee and Spirit still snoring, all made me wonder about the true history which had taken place.

It made me think of my own past years after my birth in France. My grandparents lived in Egypt where I often spent months at a time. Uganda, Lebanon, Syria, all in peaceful times. Throughout my youth I wandered those countries filled with the richness of different civilizations. A schooling in itself which I appreciated as the years went by. I was "sent here" by my Father when I was around 24 and immediately felt so comfortable living in this country. Especially in the west. More so, exactly where we were. I still debate with myself about the ramifications of an after life, which of course would bring a belief of a before life. Maybe? I have read a lot about the subject and found that there could be some truth of the spirit lingering on, not in a physical form, but as a borrowed one. I always believed I lived here before while just too comfortable and nothing of my surroundings being foreign to me even if they constantly amazed me.

Those times on the point rewarded my soul as nothing else by then mattered. What I wore, did, rich or poor. Stripped from it all I was left alone with my subconscious and my own well oiled gears. I knew the answers to my previous questions would still not surface, I also knew we would not leave being the same.

I learned of Moki Dugway and Muley Point not being far while one day in Mexican Hat. A road carved in the cliffs, one that could barely be seen from its start. How ironic it turned out to be. I listened to the man say "Three miles of unpaved switchbacks climbing 1,100 feet, a tough road to navigate on". A while back, near Moab before we broke down, I had been told Hurray Pass was an easy one. I realized I could not fully trust anyone's road description, as Moki Dugway became one of my favorite roads to ride. One we would go up and down in the middle of the night under a full moon sliding the rear wheel through those switchbacks. Quite a road so well carved into the cliff following the natural curvatures of the mountain and the view from the top exceptional. One can see Monument Valley, the Gooseneck, Valley of the Gods and the glow from the lights of Mexican Hat at night. Breathtaking, the camera lens never wide enough to capture it all. A little further, bearing to the left, a dirt road took us to Muley Point. The winning views of the area. Passed the first lookout, riding over some mild rock shelves, all together seven miles away with an elevation of 6,425 feet. The camping was free on this rocky ground where one would need boulders to secure the guy lines as stakes were useless. I started calling where I stood "My Top of the World". I could have spent the rest of my life on that point and decided this is where we would move. Sooner than later.

The weather throughout those times did not cooperate. On Gooseneck Point, the winds howled to no end forcing us back towards Bluff to the familiar Sand Island campground, same spot, different skies. We took refuge while imagining the strength of the winds on Muley Point so totally exposed, Mother Nature shutting the doors on us. Second year on the road, a second summer approaching. I could feel it in the slowly rising heat. The thought of not having a schedule did help my patience, allowing me to go with the flow as none of it was going anywhere. Hopefully not. We went through a slump. Not so much of a mental one, but physical. For the first time, my body tired out and as I looked on Spirit, I felt him needing a break as well, to rest a little longer than usual. Some, what I call, "nothing days" came upon us. Eat, sleep, read and repeat. Those nights and days did us a lot of good with plenty of food, good shelter, we only had to go three miles for water. For the first time I heard myself say "Life is good". A huge step hearing those words.

One of those days, while making a run for water, we met Joff. I did not know at the time what a "penny farthing" was, so I will call it a "strange bicycle", being exactly what I saw leaning against a mile marker post. Next to it, a skinny guy wearing an English khaki colored Bobby hat. We made a U-turn, parked next to him and realized he was as much amazed seeing us as us seeing him. We both asked each other at the same time "And what are you doing here?" His story left me speechless. The odd bicycle, this old fashioned kind with the big, or should I say, huge wheel in the front and a small one in the rear, was indeed called a penny farthing. He had almost ridden around the world during this third attempt after two knee surgeries, on a machine with no gears and one brake lever for the front wheel. We felt destined to bump into each other and exchange stories leading us to an evening at camp. In his mid-thirties, humble and kind, a young man with so much determination that I felt guilty having an engine in our vehicle. We are still in touch. He calls it, "His long ride on his big wheel". Joff Summerfield, 22,026 miles and over 924 days around the world as I read today on his website.

We have always had the good fortune to meet some stunning and over-whelming travelers. Some out for a couple days, a week, a month, some as ourselves for an undetermined lifetime. One has to move on slowly for such fortunate events to happen and the need is to see instead of just looking. On another day, when the winds slightly died down and "cabin fever" replaced the "nothing days", while going through Mexican Hat, I noticed some balloon baskets in the backs of a few pick up trucks. After some chatting, I learned that a rogue balloonist event took place every year in Valley of the Gods throughout this last weekend of April. They were leery about the winds for their meeting time the next day at six in the morning. I could not miss such an opportunity. I had seen balloons before, but never up close and personal. It would only be a 20 mile ride in the cold morning winds, or maybe no winds. They turned out to be a real nice group. A new hobby discovered, fairly simple, yet needing many friends while inflating, landing, deflating and folding, holding the lines throughout it all. I did help. Spirit did not. We had never taken much part in any activity within a crowd. This time was different. They wel-comed us with open arms as if we also were balloonists and had known each other for a long time. The next morning, under blue and magenta skies, the ground fog slowly lifting, sunrise only minutes away and no wind, they took off one at the time in a silence only broken by their blast of propane burners. The stage, already magnificent, transformed into one few words could describe, as those majestic balloons floated from one mesa to another. As time went on and the trucks with many friends followed, the winds started to pick up and each balloonist tried to land as close as possible near their support vehicle. My camera worked hard capturing all the colors of their fabric against a perfect blue sky. Flying came to a halt that day. Balloons and wind do not mix well. We met them again the next morning. Another show, unfortunately curtailed within a couple hours by more winds. On that Sunday, their ritual was a brunch in Valley of the Gods. We were invited. A bit shy at first, it did not take me too long to taste the deep fried turkey, the chocolate dipped strawberries, brisket, salads and so much more. A real treat as we were living on the road without refrigeration and here appeared this five star buffet in front of me.

Every morning the weather would start out calm and inviting for us to move to Muley Point. Within a couple hours it would never remain as such. The locals kept telling me "this was the season". I finally came to terms with a fact I did not want to confront. Moving on, no sense spending sometimes 20 hours a day in a tent. We ended up further North in the Needles. Hamburger Campground and it did not do us any good. With every blink, my eyelids polished my eyes with not so fine sand and Spirit grinding it between his teeth. We pushed on further. Moab of course, familiar, but I did not want to go back to our previous campsite. I settled, after some map searching, on Ken's Lake, a campground seven miles south of town near the start of the La Sal Mountain Loop.

All quieter there while getting some protection from the mountains. Much vegetation and peaceful with only the sound of a running creek full from the melting snow. We both took a long and deep breath. I read a nice quote from *Lao Tzu*. *"A good traveler has no fixed plans and is not intent on arriving"*. How fitting. My planning would not totally stop as it turned into more desires of destinations than anything else. As quickly pinpointed, they vaporized as if our plans were in Jell-o, another expression I overheard. On one evening, I saw a father and son pulling in not far from us on a same motorcycle as ours. He on the phone, his son listening to an iPod. A simple image taking place on the foothills of those beautiful white capped La Sal Mountains. It took me back thinking this could have been us, Lance and me. Without however the phone or iPod. I hoped they were enjoying their time to the fullest, never taking it for granted. Father's Day around the corner and even though never too often glancing at a calendar, I felt the presence of that day approaching. Acceptance and more acceptance from within. Everyone wears their own shoes, no one can see or feel inside them. More writing in our journal, pages and pages. They were my conversations with life.

Slowly but surely, good weather joined us. We remained at camp and decided to ride the La Sal Mountain loop as it seemed a perfect landscape for photos. Bright deep blue skies spotted with clouds moving right along, a masterpiece in progress. A road in great condition, a bit of snow on the banks at higher elevations and the cleanest air one could breathe. I made a little snowman at one of the pull outs where we stopped. He stood there on the hood of Spirit's sidecar under his very concerned eyes. A snowman in May. All so magnificent. We were both feeling better than ever after the much needed rest the past couple weeks. On the downhill, nearing the end of the ride, Castle Valley appeared with its own red rocks standing tall and named The Priest and the Nuns. The sun, still on the horizon, played with the colors giving them a life.

As the days lingered, we both turned a bit lazy. Rightly so I thought at the time. My senses were digging deep into this aspect of living on the road, not just traveling. Mother's Day also came by, a bittersweet one with my Mother living so far and Lance's absence. She and I did have a long conversation on the phone so glad this new so Smart Phone finally purchased worked well. There were moments feeling helpless, but the journey bared its fruit. Constantly learning to better cope with all the present emotions, sadness not anymore a bad thing but a natural sentiment. It shaped me, gave me the courage to go on as already seen so much and could not turn around. I always thought of Spirit being so understanding, our relationship getting deeper and closer. We became one on this path of ours, his eyes never ceasing his constant watch upon me. It is such a simple life with him, no demands or expectations. Lying next to me in our moments, scratching his head and belly or back, that is all we both needed. Nothing else. Those times were the gifts of life for us, they held us up with much hope for the coming future. Nothing we had started was in vain.

I truly wished everyone could have an outlet as we did. I knew without it we would have not survived the urban life. Riding is such a big part of it, a sense of freedom and adventure on paved and unpaved roads, at times visor up letting the wind blow into the full face helmet. No barriers. Summer was almost here, perfect temperatures throughout the day and a nice coolness at night. We headed south instead of north. It did not make much sense but I wanted to visit the canyons in Page, Arizona. Back through Blanding and Bluff, I waved at Valley of the Gods promising we would return, Kayenta to pick up Highway 160 and then on Highway 98 all the way to Page. We were only 250 miles away. Even though fighting more winds, the ride was a beautiful one into Navajo Reservation lands. So unprepared for Page thinking it would only be a small town, a Walmart and a Home Depot welcomed us, stores of every kind lined up, condos galore and quite a bit of traffic. We passed through and arrived at the Glen Canyon Recreation area on Lake Powell only a few miles away with much camping on its shores. I liked it. To the right, rows of RVs along the water, to the left, no one. Not a single camper. It seemed reserved for us. So perfect with fire rings, toilets and even an outdoor shower. We did not need or want to be among the shiny chrome bumpers, we had our own beach.

Anxious to visit the canyons, we stopped the next day at one of the many tour companies finding out they only catered to the upper canyon, the most popular one. I decided to start with the lower canyon called Lower Antelope Canyon or The Corkscrew. The Navajo call it Hasdeztwazi or the Spiral Rock Arches. Very unassuming as we arrived at a little shack and I could not see any entrance of a canyon. With an entry fee of $20, which I thought at the time being expensive, Spirit could not come with me. The caretakers were very kind offering to keep an eye on him while parked in the shade. For an extra $5, I signed up for the photographers tour, meaning I could stay in for as long as I wanted, even backtrack. I was not ready for the architecture Mother Nature had carved over her many years of existence. Not far from the shack, at the entrance, just a cracked opening in the ground, one would need to hang on to a well constructed metal ladder and dive down into the canyon. Figuratively that is. How can someone describe this canyon? Deep into the earth, created over thousands of years, the relentless forces of water and wind slowly carved and sculptured the multicolored sandstone into forms, textures and unimaginable shapes. One of a kind sight. Looking ahead, sometimes through the narrow passages barely wide enough for one shoe to rest on, turning around and looking behind, to the right, to the left, every square inch a showpiece. I went in with a small group and a guide, a very pleasant young man, and it did not take me long to fall behind. Trying to balance out the time spent while Spirit waited outside, I wanted to be brief, and yet take my time. One could close their eyes, point their camera and the photos would turn out worthy of printing and hanging in anyone's living room. I touched those walls, experiencing the changes of textures and colors, all so delicate that I knew no human could duplicate. The views constantly changed as the sunlight coming from above continuously dragged the shadows making any time of the day a worthy spectacle.

Visiting Upper Antelope Canyon took place the next day. We rode in an open truck with the bench seats laid out in the rear bed, pretty happy that Spirit could tag along. This canyon was fairly far from the main road through an unpaved path with deep sand. Quite different than the previous day, a true guided tour jammed with people and we needed to stay close by our guide. I missed the elegance of the Lower Canyon and ended up only taking the one photo everyone shoots for. The one where the light rays shine in from a hole in the ceiling on the angle of the moment while the guide throws some sand in the air. This is after having to elbow and push myself to the front, the "professional" photographers with their tripods not wanting to share a single square inch of their space. A disappointing feeling like being in the middle of a herd of cattle led not from the sound of a bell, but at least, a bit better, the melody from a flute. We have since been back a few times to only experience the lower canyon.

Without too much warning, Father's Day came around. I wanted to just blink and make it go away, but how cowardly would that be? Test day. I filed that one as such. *"It is through pain one gains wisdom"* I kept repeating. An ancient quote from the Mayan culture. How much more wisdom did I need throughout that day unable to live in the moment. The emotions too strong, I could not even feel and see the beauty surrounding us while still camping on the shores of Lake Powell. A day of confrontation with myself coming to the conclusion to let those hours go by without a fight, happy and sad all at the same time. Simply human to feel as such. I wrote more words in our journal that day while also wishing all our readers a Happy Father's Day.

How well will I always remember the summer of 2008? Always. Fuel crunch time, the prices soared to above $5 a gallon. With five gallons in the tank and another ten in two separate spare Jerry cans, the total gave us a range of about 300 miles, 350 with a good tail wind, all for close to $60. A tight fit in the budget if we wanted to eat. I decided to head north as the shores of Lake Powell were starting to gain momentum on the temperature chart. One look at the topographic map, close to 6,000 feet, the little town of Escalante with a population of 1,000 became our base camp. We checked into a very vacant little RV park. Nice flat ground in the back, in a corner, bathrooms with showers, laundromat, wifi, electricity and water, all for a very low monthly fee. I think the owner felt sorry for us, or maybe for Spirit. We had to wait for the fuel prices to come down and were not going to ride every day. For that matter, I decided at the most a couple times a week. It turned out to be a great decision. We lived in cooler weather, walked to town, and to this day even after idling for a few months, we still have not explored the entire area.

I picked a weekly route counting the miles. There were so many being in the middle of it all, right on Highway 12, one of the ten scenic byways of the country on the edges of the Grand Staircase National Monument. A perfect scenario even if fuel would have been affordable. We got lucky with time on our side. One of our first rides, to Wide Hollow Reservoir, not too far while waiting for a new seal. The bearings seal at the rear wheel started leaking and I did not want to push our luck. Peaceful reservoir, the water calm with its own little beach on one end, a perfect space for us to spend the day. A good book, food, Spirit running around, who cared about the fuel prices. In the meantime, I kept an eye on a fire burning 15 miles away and only 20% contained by 365 firefighters. I begged Mother Nature to be kind with her winds and spare us all. She listened. I really did not want to move.

The seal arrived taking only a few minutes to change, thanks to much advice on the Internet from a motorcycle forum. Next, the Petrified Forest, such timber always being a riddle for me. The best one ever experienced, especially with Spirit being allowed on the trails. Getting used to the altitude, we easily climbed the 200 steps leading to the top. A good hike for us which I thought we should do more often. It would keep us both in good shape. It did not take long to come across the inconceivable displays of petrified wood. Both the quantity and quality impressed me. Hundreds of millions of years ago, a huge river flowed through the area and periodically flooded. One of those floods must have been very violent, as it ripped up the trees from a nearby forest, washed them downstream and piled them in a sort of prehistoric log jam. They were of all colors laying every few steps, some even protruding out of the ground all along with some great scenery of the area. I read a sign which said the petrified wood was supposedly haunted and stealing some pieces would bring bad luck. I could not help touching them being mesmerized by such ancient artifacts right in front of me. Another wonder of Mother Nature, another process so unlike the canyons just visited. Petrified wood literally means wood turned into stone. They are remains of a terrestrial vegetation and is the amazing result of a tree, or tree-like plant, having been completely transitioned to stone by the process of permineralization. The organic materials have been replaced with minerals, mostly a silicate such as quartz, retaining the original structure of the stem tissue. Fascinating aspects surrounding us. One thinking it is wood, but is not. The colors were intense and each a bit different from the other because of its contaminating elements. Black was carbon, green and blue were cobalt, chromium and copper, red, brown and yellow were iron oxides, pink and orange were manganese.

The new seal held up fine. I could see no leakage, and the following week we went on further with our fuel allotment. We both were on an allowance with no complaint from either of us. We arrived in Boulder, just a curve in the road while riding Highway 12, one I could have enjoyed every day. The elevations are around 8,000 to 9,000 feet, the grades anywhere between eight and 14%. On one stretch, sheer cliffs on each side and a vision of total emptiness as far as one could see. We met another roadside attraction. An even greater oddity, Joe, rollerblading from San Francisco to his home town, Ocean City in Maryland. I knew it right away before our U-turn, seeing a different set-up. A man sitting on the side of the road with a pair of roller blades next to him and parked on the side, a baby carriage, one of those high tech ones with a front disc brake to slow him down while going downhill. Quite simple as it gave him much room to store his gear, including food and water. He had to my amazement, crossed Australia the year before, and now only left him with two more months to reach his destination before starting photo journalism school. I promised myself I would never again complain about a backache or a cross wind.

I ended up getting a job at the Boulder Trail Grill. Right on the corner of Highway 12 and the beginning of Burr Trail. While stopped there, treating myself to one of those rare eating out lunches, one conversation led to another regarding help they much needed. I would be the one. I thought. Very dog friendly restaurant with a fenced back yard, three days a week, the pay adequate for those times. Anything to help out with extra fuel. I could easily make grilled chicken quesadillas, hamburgers and cheeseburgers. Especially with no fryer, as the owner thought a too messy way to cook. Bags of chips thrown in the basket made it even easier. Unfortunately it did not last long and I was let go within a couple weeks, meaning I got fired. The manager, a newbie with maybe at the most one year of experience, myself a chef for over 40 years, we radically tangled. My invaluable lesson? I should have kept my mouth shut. All I could say was, "let's do it this way, let's do it that way" meaning, let's do it my way. It did not go over very well and she quickly reported me to the owner for insubordination as her insecurity could not handle me very well. The owner, a very kind lady, apologized profusely. She could not fire the manager as I did not want a full time job, giving her only one choice. Thus my experience in Boulder. The few dollars and free meals did not hurt.

Boulder was at the start of another most beautiful ride we would experience many times. It begins at the Burr Trail, paved through a deep and winding canyon, turns into a very mild and doable unpaved road, on to some incredible switchbacks where when ending one can make a left on Notom Road, already part of Capitol Reef National Park, or a right continuing towards Lake Powell. I knew too well by then, there would never be such a thing as "my favorite", but that road is on the top ten for me. I turned 60 that day while within that space. Best gift I could ever receive besides an early morning call from my dear Mother, as usual worried about me. I also celebrated Spirit's birthday. As no one at the shelter knew his birth date, he and I would have it on the same day. Four and still such a puppy! It was also my 300th entry in my journal, surprised I had written so much. There were many lessons already contained within those pages. In retrospect, mostly peaceful times and constant discoveries of one's self, life, emotions, upward steps. That ride, that day, it made it all even more special.

Perfect cooler temperatures, a nice breeze and puffy clouds. The first mile or so out of Boulder, the road became lined with carpets of blue flowers on each side swaying in the winds. Empty of dwellings, the grounds like welcoming banners. The next miles were imposing former sand dunes. One called the Sugarloaf. Hard to believe that at one time all sand. It had taken millions of years. Mother Nature works slowly. Masterpieces take time. Adorned by large cross-bedding patterns, the Sugarloaf was caused by the eolian, or wind blown, depositions of sand dunes which were repeatedly buried and exposed in cycles over time. The joinings in the sandstone were the result of continuous cracking related to slow changing of pressure. A little campground appeared on the left with a multitude of trees present and I knew there must have been a creek running nearby. Good spot for lunch, sheltered from the sun, cozy space and a bit tight. We found the creek and a sign which said "Access road, private land, do not block". It confused me being placed on the main path and wanting to find out why. The makeshift road stopped at the creek, the bank across a dead end. I later found out one would need to make a right into the creek itself and a bit further, the main path would again pick up across the bank. We did not have quite the proper vehicle for it as I previously learned my lesson. Instead, we enjoyed a pleasant lunchtime. A bit further, a steep downhill and to my left, as we reached a half way point lookout, I could see this grandiose canyon. I remember whistling to myself. Into the red canyon, long time ago, a river ran where the present road now existed and each curve eroded deeply into the rocks. Not a single car, not another human being in the vicinity. I wanted to stop everywhere and walk the road. Why even ride it? At the same time, being our first pass, curious to see further. And so we did, as we arrived where the pavement ended and a ribbon of dirt continued into the horizon. We went ahead and as all happens always so fast even when so slow, a few miles further, I looked down at some of the most beautiful switchbacks ever seen.

"It is a lovely and terrible wilderness, harshly and beautifully colored, broken and worn until its bones are exposed. And in hidden corners and pockets under its cliffs the sudden poetry of Spring" ~ Wallace Stegner ~ "Wilderness Letters, 1960".

We were now on Capitol Reef National Park land savoring those switch-backs. Arriving at the bottom, we did not make a right or a left. Those roads would have to wait for another day. Time passed by quickly with too many stops for photos and the long pleasant lunch. Northbound, Capitol Reef stood 48 miles away, southbound, Bullfrog Basin, 33 miles as the map showed upon our return. Through it all, Spirit always the best companion. He never minded where we went, I never asked him. Eat, sleep, ride and play. The perfect life for my buddy. I have said I want to be him if I ever come back some day. It began some serious research and highlighting on the map that night with so much around us and we were truly fortunate our path brought us here to stay. On the map, I found a ghost town named Widstoe. It would be an interesting ride going northwest of Escalante on Main Canyon Road, numbered 118. I was never sure of the names or numbers, every map being different including the BLM office with its own version. Quite a change of scenery while riding through Dixie National Forest. Strangely eerie, blackened by the fire, most of the trees and grounds still smoldering here and there. We passed the burned out area and arrived at an intersection which did not appear on my map or GPS. Five choices of roads while ahead of us stood a small size meadow covered with flowers of all colors. No need for a decision. Lunch time. We just laid there among the flowers watching the world go by. Not a bad life I thought while feeling I had climbed a couple steps without falling backwards. I wondered if it was due to aging? Some realizations one has when the years are coming up in numbers. It is what it is. Embracing the moments, trying to rewind the good memories, the ones that made me smile, even laugh.

Back on the saddle, which road to take? I numbered them logically as when one goes up and reaches a summit, one must come down. I picked number two. A good choice. The area was deserted for miles on end and as usual the day moving on a bit faster than my liking. We never found the ghost town, instead arrived on the main road. I brought up the website after our return, and found out the ghost town remained in pretty bad shape having been totally abandoned since 1936, after the government bought it and placed the land under the provisions of the Taylor Grazing Act. Disappointed, we had missed it by only a couple hundred feet when by the cemetery, I did not make the needed left turn.

The good life in Escalante continued. The price of fuel did not come down, but slightly went up while reading on the Internet about its cost skyrocketing in Death Valley and California, way above seven dollars a gallon. Through some motorcycle forums, I sadly found out many riders even stopped taking joy rides. Hand in hand, the price of food also went up at the only grocery store in town where everyone gathered on Tuesdays, delivery day. Not much ever made it to the shelves as we all rummaged through the incoming boxes of fresh produce and whatever else needed. In contrast, the rental RVs seemed to be all over the roads driving at warp speeds, as most likely the Europeans thought they were still on the Autobahn. They appeared taking advantage of the falling dollar exchange and pumping a bit of money into this local economy which surrounded us. It was not inexpensive anymore to be on the road, even with a motorcycle. We were fine though. We continued being able to afford this little space at the end of town with all the comforts and rides which by then dropped down to once a week. This too shall pass I kept thinking. Unless of course we became permanent residents, but winter in Escalante in a tent would not be much fun.

Mid-July arrived. The hottest time of the year, more so the day I decided to explore Kodachrome Basin Park. To make matters worse, I forgot my backpack, meaning I could not carry much water. Too late to go back, too many miles, I settled for a short hike. We would leave the longer ones for another day. They described the park as a "Mystery in Stone". The main paved road leading to the park only a couple miles long, hiking a must to appreciate the surroundings. Present, a little store, some cabins and even horse rentals. Nice spring water from a faucet as I managed to hang a couple bottles from my belt. Spirit's bowl also missing, I would use my cap as a makeshift solution. Things were not so bad after all, but did not go as well as I thought. On the short hike through the canyon lined by beautiful and colorful red sandstone rocks, the temperature rose by at least ten degrees. I knew Spirit would have a real hard time walking on that hot sand, not happy having to jump from shade to shade. We did try boots for him at some point, but he could not walk with them on, which turned into a very funny show watching him so awkwardly tiptoeing right along like a ballerina. The boots only lasted a few minutes. So we took it slow as we arrived at the half way point when this situation arose. I followed him from shade to shade, no sense turning around as the distance would have been the same. Intriguing, dramatic and striking, Mother Nature had one more time outdone herself. Back at the store we borrowed a bowl, found some shade to park under and Spirit felt much better. I left him behind for a short walk of less than a mile through the Nature Trail. A paved man-made trail. Very nicely done and very informative like a walk through history, geology and science books all at the same time. The pointed rocky formations are called "pipes", also known as "sedimentary pipes". They range from the middle Jurassic to the upper Cretaceous period, all between 95 to 180 million years ago. There were 67 of them, each quite a sight. They looked like cone heads. The heat tired me as I came back and sat with Spirit before one last short ride to the Shakespeare Arch Trail, where a giant pipe, the widest and tallest of them all, gave us more than enough shade.

July in Utah. I never thought about heading north even if we could afford it. I wanted to be stuck in Escalante and its surroundings. Here and there a bit warm, doable, and so we stayed. A rider from San Diego arrived and camped near us. Pete. An interesting character. One of those that fabricates "things". He pulled his off-road bike along with his street bike on a homemade trailer. A 1974 Honda Sabre followed by a Suzuki DR350. What a sight to see them rolling down the road! He had planned one month away from his home in Santa Cruz and I had never seen anyone pack so much gear. Everything homemade, including a hydraulic tongue shaft for his trailer so it would not rear end his bike when stopping. With a smile on my face I discovered his dual handlebars on the Honda. One set for city riding and one more relaxed for those long highway stretches. I think he waited for me to criticize him, but, why not? I did not, all made so much sense. With one aspect in common, looks did not matter, as long as it worked and did the job. He is the one who showed me the right way to change a tire, and maybe the not so proper way to inflate it. Throwing a match into a few drops of lighter fluid sprayed into the tire. Hair spray would also work he said, just make sure your valve is removed. We did it and it worked. In reality, he did it and it worked, after I took a couple steps back.

We rode the 38 miles of Hell's Backbone Road together, and my kidneys felt each turn of the wheel. Built in the 1930's by the Civilian Conservation Group, before Scenic Highway 12 was laid out, the road joined Escalante to Boulder and traveled by the mail couriers with their mules. The last route in the country used by such couriers. Unpaved, with the worse washboards ever experienced, it only gave us a choice of either going fast or real slow. Pete picked up the speed while I dropped mine way down. The must see was the bridge which joined two mountain peaks at 9,000 feet. 109 feet long, 14 feet wide with a drop of 1,500 feet on each side. Quite an accomplishment for that time period to build such a bridge which offered those spectacular views. That is the way I like to ride with others. Everyone at their own speed within their own comfort zone. Pete waited for us by the bridge where we took a long break. I loved the trees growing right out of the rocks. I called them "Mother Nature's furniture". Beautiful weathered colors, some limbs broken from the harsh winters, others standing strong while wrapping themselves around any hard surface they could find for anchor. The campsites in the area were many. Torn between staying at our present site or moving. I got lazy and we stayed in Escalante. I did not want to abandon the free showers! I also started wondering if I was getting a bit softer.

Pete's departure took place. Content about his stay, he explored on his own some roads we could not ride, the ones needing a true off road motorcycle. We always kept a nice space between us, never crowding each other and so pleasant to have conversations with another soul. Alone again, my own realizations came back to mind. I started slipping a bit. Curled up in a corner awaiting my own time never an option. The peaks were always so bright, the valleys I would fall into were at times too dark. I found an envelope filled with Lance's photographs. I knew they were there. I also knew of my avoidance. A tear and a smile. Always, while looking at him. Such an innocent and beautiful young man with his black hair and green eyes. I kept feeling like an ostrich burying my head in the sand. My sand was the road, new ones, unfamiliar ones. Sometimes I thought of it not being right, others times, what I needed to do. Often, just torn in between.

We could not move. Not yet. The price of fuel and food became a waiting game, daily checking the boards. Even the once a week ride became a hard aspect on the wallet. We often just walked to town and mingled a bit with the locals. I wished I had been smarter about the job, it would have helped a lot. Instead, my Mother helped us out in the form of a late birthday present. We did not go too far, about 100 miles through Torrey to Capitol Reef. A good move much needed. Sometimes I thought of it as being unfortunate because of so much more to explore around Escalante. Often, I could not comprehend my ways, I just followed them. As long as they made me feel better and radiated some sunshine in our days, that is what I needed to do. Spirit always agreed. Camping became a bit pricier and more crowded. Capitol Reed, a center for tourists to stop. I saw it all as bargaining with the present times. We could not have it all day in and day out. Magnificent sights were present. Chimney Rock, Twin Rocks, the Castle, the historical district of Fruita and its Petroglyphs, Hickman Bridge, Capitol Dome, Orientation Pull Out. An endless list and the destinations so close, all under some great weather, Capitol Reef so rich in culture. It had been a homeland for thousands of years.

The canyons served as the perfect path for the hunters and the gatherers while on their migrations. The Fremont culture solidified around 500 BC, from food foraging groups to eventually farmers of corn, beans and squash. In the 1800's, more explorers arrived and so did Mormon pioneers settling in the Fruita Rural Historical District. They planted orchards of apples, pears, peaches, apricots, mulberries, cherries and even Pottawatomie plums which all still present.

We rode Capitol Reef Road and the Grand Wash to its dead end. All this new to me, culture, nature, geology and more, made me feel alive. We were right in the Waterpocket Fold which defined the area for 100 miles as a classic monocline. Intense learning having never heard of a monocline before. A "step-up" in the rock layers as on the west side lifted more than 7,000 feet higher than the layers on the east side. Always hard to believe how my surroundings were formed. Sometimes I questioned the fact it all happened between 50 and 200 million years ago. Such a vast slice of time so inconceivable to me. More rocks from the Permian to the Cretaceous ages went as far back as 250 million years. Yet, all present along the unpaved roads with the camera taking pictures and Spirit, truthfully not knowing his thoughts but looking pretty happy. We maybe spent too much time alone and now enjoyed being in a campground with others around us. It could have been the crowd being respectful of noises, nice people truly interested in the area, or could it have just been me? It did not matter. We met a couple from the Netherlands and chatted for a while. Later on, their two children were looking at Spirit from a distance and whispering in each other's ear. I knew they were being shy and I called them over. Spirit loves children, people and other animals. They kept him busy for a while, good for him to socialize with his tail wagging as always. I felt so strongly we were back on our road. With a moon almost full and coming up, while at the same time sunset taking place, we took a ride into the Grand Wash. I lived for those moments. They are the ones that helped me climb the staircase that stared at me daily. I kept repeating a quote a reader of ours had sent us: *"Today is the first day of the rest of your life" [Charles Dederich].* We were exactly where we needed to be. I gave myself permission to go on.

A friend of mine was coming to Moab. Paul. I had never put on any miles to meet anyone, but Paul and I with a common denominator needed to meet. A reader of our journal for quite a while and always very supportive of us through e-mails and telephone calls. When this last Father's day arrived, I received a very generous and friendly e-mail from him. That Sunday went by and as Monday came along, I saw another e-mail from him. One which to this day leaves me so emotional. His daughter Alyssa, in a car accident the night before, had passed away. Seventeen years old. A beautiful young lady. This came from a man so considerate of our own path. What does one say? As myself I had heard it all. All the cliché quotes and thoughts, which I knew were meant well within those moments of such a tragic loss, but no words truly with any meaning whatsoever. *"I am here for you"* were mine to him as he replied some time later *"I am just one who has lost his taste buds and cannot savor the delightful flavors that were once daily experiences. In sailor's terms, I have hit the doldrums, no winds in my sails, but every now and then a good current comes along and moves me into a fresh breeze".* I wished so much I could divert him some of our wind to his sails. To be there for each other was the best we could do. He riding twice our distance while coming from Chicago, Moab, even though would be a bit warm, seemed a good place to meet. We settled on a campground at the north end of town. One with much comfort as we would be sharing a space.

The weather ended up being brutal, but if I had to do it again, I would. Two men sharing the same loss, unexplained as it will remain, both of us trying our hardest to deal with a situation too often uncontrollable. Saying interesting conversations took place would be an understatement. Candid words and emotions surfaced which only we could understand. Paul, younger than me, self employed, married with one more daughter, he seemed to have a better grasp on life's unfairness than I did with a busier journey than us, an immediate family support system which lacked on our roads. As we parted a few days later, I saw him more as a solid rock and myself as a sandstone still eroding and taking shape.

To my own surprise, we returned to Escalante. Like a magnet, the space called us back. Same little campsite out of the way, they were glad to see us back. We started having visitors, friends known for a while before our departure, everyone on their own destinations. Louis from Canada, an accomplished rider and a born comedian. Tomas and Marianne throughout their car camping trip from Denver and Brian from Florida once met in Terlingua. We must all have been at the right place at the right time, as if and when planning, such visits generally never work out while on the road. Good food and conversations, many memories brought back. As quickly as they came, they also left. We revisited Bryce Canyon, this time without the snow and the past colder temperatures. We stopped again at every pull out. It took us all day, and my mood in the late afternoon went downhill when a ranger told me that dogs were not allowed in the parking lots. More precisely, they were not allowed out of the vehicles, even on a leash. Blown away I asked for the reason. They disturbed the chipmunks and the ravens that tourists like so much to photograph. Dogs were allowed in the campgrounds and on the roads branching out from the main one, those according to the regulations. We left. I could not comprehend such an idiotic aspect. I still don't.

We so much settled into our journey. Besides such an incident as above, all flowing with ease even if the finances seemed tight. I got used to it. We lived a whole month on what I made in one day when I worked. The country became our home and the roads its hallways. They were the common real estate for everyone. Those strips of black top or dirt, designed to go from point A to point B, sand or gravel, washboards, ruts and rocks all included. They started to take on a different image and meaning having a life of their own, reverberating feelings enjoyed or disregarded by many in ways numbering the human personalities. Their shoulders and pull outs became the most interesting areas where we would often stop, take out my chair and watch everyone going by. At times, others would stop, they became meeting points. We met many different characters riding their motorcycles and bicycles, driving their cars, even walking. Some so proud to display their expensive and well set up vehicles kept immaculate as if they stopped every mile to wipe them down. Others, as myself, experienced them as tools, hoping for their mechanical ability to take them to that point B they were in route to. Some purposely noisy as to turn many heads while trying to express a certain sense of superiority. A few quiet ones accelerating at warp speeds when leaving, thus stimulating one's heart rate with their musical tones of an engine well tuned up. Most with moments dictated by a schedule, a clock they stayed in synch with. It became common for me to hear after they would find out we lived on the road "Someday, I will also…"

Late August arrived. We fell into September and had not yet ventured north of Utah. The colder days at our elevation not too far away and we made a beeline to The Oasis in Texas. Straight down, as all of a sudden, I just wanted to be "there". I never believed in owning land feeling it only being a privilege to possess its title. This time around however, I thought "It is mine and no one could disturb us from it". After so many destinations, sometimes a bit isolated, more often than not surrounded by many, this piece of land became a welcome sight. It is still as such today. Our readers kept daily sending us ideas on how to live besides in a tent and also met locals each with a different opinion and suggestions for a dwelling. I picked the easiest choice. An older 23 foot RV. The present my Mother had talked about in earlier months. Total luxury for us as I managed to install more solar power. With the shipping container, its water catchment, a phone and an internet line, while further expanding the fire ring, my Center of the Universe, The Oasis became for us very livable. 660' × 660' = 10 acres. My Mother's generous present.

Winter wanted us to only stay in the shadows. The surrounding horizons wide open as far as one could see with the most beautiful sunrises and sunsets. Under the full moon we could ride without headlights and on darker nights, the blanket of stars and the Milky Way always so present. At times, with a heavy heart, my thoughts on the shady side, my channels mixed up and too much static filled the screen forcing me to stare at, becoming merely a particle of sand within this vast universe surrounding us. Other days, the glow of the sunshine, the often great weather, exploring the endless roads, all opened up the door towards a frame of mind slowly healing. I did not want to stay confused and left hanging by some thin threads creating this vertigo which would sway me into a space I wanted to escape. I fought hard. I felt so human those upcoming months while facing an undisturbed reality. Nothing could have been more real. Just Spirit and me.

A reader of our journal wrote me *"Lance will be with you always in spirit. To have known such a love in life is all we can ask for! Think of the millions of people who will spend their whole life never knowing the kind of love shared between you two. We are all here but for a brief moment in the space of time to enjoy what God has granted us to experience. Your words in "The Oasis of my Soul" profoundly relays your undying love for him and know this… there is a window from above that we are all being viewed from as mere mortals on earth. A window where he is there, watching over you, waiting for the day you can be together again! In your heart you know this already! Until then you have Spirit as your co-pilot and what a wonderful journey you still have ahead of you".* I had to see beyond my own present stage and change the props surrounding my inner thoughts. I worked on it with the knowledge of the few quiet months left ahead of us.

The days started to blend in. Ever so slowly as again any notion of time disappeared. Part of me missed the road, but we were happy to be here. So much silence. Only sometimes, depending on the direction of the wind, I could hear the rare truck or car traveling on Highway 118. Lance's birthday was coming up. Hard to believe a whole year had gone by. I was the one supposed to give him a gift, instead, I felt The Oasis being his gift and wish. This is where he and I, for now, would be together. Our own undisturbed space. We floated freely with no boundaries, no hold on us as I never set any parameters. Mother Nature remained our mistress, always so generous. The present stillness possessed a different call than the movement we were used to. I leaned into the tranquility which provided everything we both needed. Reflections were many as the outside world stopped interfering with our life. Big Bend National Park remained our favorite destination whenever I decided to roll on down the road. Something still happens to me as we cross the gate. Its vastness always overwhelming and being the least visited park in the country, traffic often nonexistent.

We walked a lot, or should I call it hiking? There are many unpaved roads around us. The morning and evening hours a daily gift for us and sometimes for the camera. Flowers whose names I did not know started to bloom. Plants of all shapes and colors, many being cactuses, always on our path. A good winter. Spirit also changed. He so much enjoyed being off his leash and knew his boundaries. His clowning increased. The jumping dog as I called him. My shadow through the nights and days never leaving my sight. When he napped, if I moved even as little as five feet, his eyes would open making sure I did not go too far. If I did, he would move. Besides it all, he just worked on his tan while happily dreaming.

Storms made their way down from the north. For as many years as I lived on a sailboat always on the alert, there were a couple instances when preparedness escaped me. Maybe inattention? Too much faith in the constant good weather and disregarding the forecast? The grounds would turn to mud as their first few inches soft and powdery, down below, hard limestone. The all weather road leading to the main artery became impassable. We anchored down a few times when cabin fever would then surface. There is only so much I can read, write, cook, eat and sleep. Those days never lasted too long, just a reminder of stages we escaped from the northern spaces. Staying still, reflections about life became many while going down memory lane. Thinking about my youth in Europe, my grandparents in Egypt and so much time spent with them, my years attending culinary school in Switzerland. Many kind e-mails showed up. It seemed I unintentionally helped others also grieving, giving them the courage to confront reality, or some just locked in their own cubicles plowing through their workdays. A couple hate mails came as well. They initially upset me greatly, insulting the memory of Lance. Were they real human beings? Who were they? I never got a reply as cowardly they used disposable e-mail addresses. I painfully never understood why anyone with such a mean streak would even take the time to read our journal. Those couple e-mails pushed me further back into a corner where I felt more comfortable than ever. Live and let live. My plate already full, there was no sense trying to bite others and lower myself to a standard so absent. With much incomprehension, I took it as being part of a different reality of this life wandered through. This short journey.

October 13th, 2008. The images resurfaced. So close and yet so far. My mind had such an ability to transport itself back in time, so vividly, so true to form. I remembered, one at a time, the brightly lit birthday cakes, the past gifts and the laughter. Each being a part of this giant puzzle which came together as the day went on while sitting by the fire pits, that Center of my Universe where his name I had written in stones, and as time passing by, the weather slowly embedded them in the soil. I did smile all day. I smiled from the fear that Lance would be watching me and become upset if I did not. It was always the last thing he would have wanted me to be, sad. I held his photos close by me and one more time, my eyes rested on each of them. Every part of his body came alive. It made me smile even more. I lit some large candles that evening and stayed up all night trying to find him in the many shooting stars passing by. My yearly ritual.

We confronted a mechanical breakdown. The clutch started slipping on Old Faithful in fourth and fifth gear. My friend Paul from a few miles up the road told me to bring it over. He would take care of the repair after I ordered the new parts. Never one with much mechanical ability, I did not comprehend manuals. I only knew the basic maintenance learned in years past when a mechanic invited me to his house for a weekend teaching. Valve adjustments, throttle bodies, rocker arms, how to properly change the oils, brake pads, clutch cable. Paul's knowledge went much deeper as he also wrote mechanical articles for magazines. It took us three days to change the clutch. I say "us", but it was actually just him, as I, more than anything else watched, not even fast enough to hand him the tools. I learned much. Not how to change a clutch, but the logic, the patience and perseverance behind the mechanical aspects of fixing, changing, tuning. He would always say *"It is only a matter of nuts and bolts"*. It is a knowledge I still carry with me today and has saved me so many times from giving up on much needed projects. I learned to pass on the help received, money never being the carrot dangling in front of our noses. We did it to help each other out. An aspect that overflowed into my own life toward others on my path who needed help. Along a great time, I got to know the man behind the wrenches. A good man. A "human fix".

I watched the weather all around the country. Besides Florida, we were the only state with some decent temperatures. It would freeze at times during the nights, and wore short sleeve T-shirts by noon as the sun pumped much needed power into the solar system. A repeat of past winters. Much happened some days, nothing other ones. The luxury of free time surfaced. Morning sunrises over a nice cup of coffee seemed the norm as well as the long sunsets with the clouds and colors changing on a seat facing west. We were just "being in the now".

I did not call The Oasis "Home". Not yet. I could not bring myself to do such as my only desire and need was to be on the road as two vagabonds, gypsies, whatever one could call us. I called it our base camp for a long time. A perfect one. A winter stopover recharging our own inner batteries and thinking about future destinations when the weather up north would change. I wanted so much to camp within those cold and snowy spaces. As a friend reminded me however, its romance sounded wonderful, but its winter camping reality harsh. I knew that. Nothing wrong with dreaming. So we stayed. These ten acres which seemed so immense when we first arrived started shrinking. On the east, a few others moved in. Little white dots were taking shape. They were in the sunrise photos of Nine Points. Fortunately no one moved west of us, the better view, the sunset view.

I read about the *"Power of Silence"*. A passage edited by *Kent Nerburn* from Native American wisdom. *"We believe profoundly in silence, the sign of a perfect equilibrium. Silence is the absolute poise or balance of body, mind and spirit. Those who can preserve their self-hood ever calm and unshaken by the storms of existence, not a leaf as it were, a stir on the tree, not a ripple upon the shining pool, those in the mind of the person of nature, possess the ideal attitude and conduct of life. If you ask 'What are the fruit of silence?', we will answer, 'They are self-control, true courage and endurance, patience, dignity and reverence. Silence is the cornerstone of character'"*.

Those words kept me company. In the skies, always a bird or two, on the ground, sometimes the quiet passage of a coyote, a rabbit running across an imaginary lane, crickets talking, more coyotes at night when surrounding us while the packs would howl at each other. The cycle repeated itself continuously, as did ours. I thought at times about moving to Austin or some other big city, where I could get a job which would help us out once we headed north again. That thought never materialized. We had come too far along in our ways to go back to that lifestyle. It did not cost much to be here. As for the future? Whatever happened, would happen. In the meantime, those surrounding three million acres kept us busy when we wanted to be. Back into the park we often rode to the Boquillas lookout. That little abandoned town in Mexico, as then the crossing of the Rio Grande was not yet allowed. The deep sand of Old Marathon Road dropping us into another area of the same park, more camping at the Chinati Hot Springs, the very dog friendly State Park, Indian Trail Head reminding me of Utah's geology. So much more. We visited some neighbors and met new ones on the Porch in Terlingua. Explored the ghost town of Shafter, the little artsy city of Marfa again, Marathon and Fort Davis. We even spent a few days in the Texas Hill Country. Hiked Closed Canyon a few times and the banks of the Rio Grande. We spent Thanksgiving Day at the Cowhead Ranch a few miles up the road and Christmas at The Oasis where I invited a few neighbors for a stew and homemade bread. Their own presents taking us to Terlingua Creek with a couple trucks and gathering some rocks to enlarge my Center of the Universe. They were all good times. I could not believe how fast all passed us by as January and a new year arrived so quickly.

With Spring on its way it was time to move on. Not much to do but leave it all behind, all that "stuff" which made our life easier. The shipping container, Big Green Giant as I called it, became handy. Everything stored, locked, and on we went, base camp being abandoned for a few months with no idea when we would return. It is how we lived and still do. The both of us, free spirits, nights and days both together. While on our way out, I looked back a few times and stopped a couple miles away when we approached Highway 118, torn between the thirst of the road and the love for that solitude already left behind. The land would wait for us. I knew that much. Spending a summer on it was not conceivable, not with the upcoming temperatures. We arrived in Alpine and I still did not know where we were going, the start of a habit of mine never quite knowing a precise destination. I remembered seeing photos of the Carlsbad Caverns, New Mexico, all new to us, as were the roads leading to it. Most of them. Highway 17 to Fort Davis, Balmorhea, arriving in Pecos, then on Highway 285 all the way to Carlsbad. I didn't know what to expect. Free camping absent, I found a desolate out of the way campground where a few RVs seemed to have been there for a while. I found out the next morning, at the entrance of the caverns, that dogs were not allowed in. Fortunately, they had a little kennel for that purpose, as I was not going to leave Spirit in the sidecar for the length of time it would take me throughout my tour. I disliked kennels so much. This would be the first time I went that route. I did not even want to look back at his eyes when I walked away.

Carlsbad Cavern is only one of over 300 limestone caves in a fossil reef laid down by a sea island 250 to 280 million years ago. Camera and this time tripod in hand, I started the self guided tour. One of those once in a lifetime experiences. How could a reef be of such an immense size I kept thinking. How could this cavern be one of 300 others? How many drops of rain water traveled down from the above ground surface, to finally arrive into these open spaces and leave behind the limestone which shaped the stalactites and stalagmites? Along smooth walkways downhill into the different chambers, lights installed of all different colors and close to a million bats lined the ceilings, every step an amazing sight. Nothing like I'd seen or experienced before. The tour dropped 750 feet below the surface. The names of the chambers kept appearing: Balloon Ballroom, Chocolate High, King's Palace, so many more. The park itself contained 118 caves and only three open to the public, with so far, 120 miles of passages explored and documented. Mind blowing, transported once again into a stage at times so totally incomprehensible.

I took too many photos that day. I could not help it. I wanted to look back at them and remember this now familiar acquaintance. At the same time, Spirit was on my mind, so used to having him as my shadow, awkward without him as I am sure he also felt as such. I saw the elevators manned by a ranger. A good sight, dreading the walk back uphill camera and tripod in hand, all against the incoming foot traffic. I became claustrophobic in the cabin and it seemed that when the ranger explained this would be similar to going up a 72 story building, I turned a bit pale. He asked me if I was alright. I told him I would have done better without such information! He only smiled. Spirit and I reunited, both happy, his tail wagging as usual, his head rubbing against my legs, a habit of his he also does with others. A sign of affection.

A few days later, Carlsbad behind us, we found ourselves back in Utah, our routes not surprising me anymore. The decisions always made at the last minute, sometimes turning around after a few miles, some inner voice telling me to go the other way. I called it the "ultimate freedom". Arriving north of St. George had its reason. My friend Michael e-mailed us asking to join him for some destinations he wanted to share. He and I always rode well together, meaning we did not ride side by side and only met at a designated point by the end or during the day. As we met, he gave me a couple names. Golden Butte Road and Whitney Pocket. I did not want any details. I like the element of surprise and my trust toward him was 100%. The man knew his State and the ones adjacent to it. While retired, he had done much exploration into many unknown areas. The ones tourists would not and could not reach. We arrived together in Mesquite as we left Utah the next day after crossing a few miles of Arizona and Nevada. From Mesquite we took West Riverside Road which is also Highway 170 and made a left on Golden Butte Road. Twenty-six miles of some not so good unpaved roads and the scenery did not excite me much. I wondered why we had taken that road, even asked him while we stopped for a break. I got a big smile back and just a few words "wait and you will see". Who was I to argue? With flat and non-descriptive terrain on both sides, we continued as the day got a bit warmer. It came time to make a right turn as Michael waited for us. I did not like the condition of that road. Two miles only he said. I instead dismounted and hiked a couple hundred feet to check it out and found it to be doable. Not by choice, only for what waited. Bumpy, rocky, a few washes and many ruts from the recent rains. Not a road we would have ridden in normal circumstances by ourselves. I thought about the fact we would be returning the same way, and where by then would the sidecar wheel be? Always the tricky part about being on three wheels versus two, or four for that matter. We arrived in one piece at the sight. Out of nowhere, a mount of rocks of all colors surrounded by Joshua trees as sentinels keeping vigil. Others had been here before us. Assembled fire rings were present.

Whitney Pocket impacted me much that day. We took a circular hike around it and ended up crawling through a window in the rocks which led to a chamber with no roof and walls covered with Petroglyphs. The colors streaked with moss of shades never seen before. From yellows to mauves, magentas and all in between. This is what Michael wanted me to experience. I crawled through that opening as I crawled through life those past years so much in touch with the environment, maybe too much sometimes. I knew many would only see these rocks as photos and memories. I saw them that day in direct correlation with my own life filled with unimaginable shapes and colors, textures each so different as the days of this journey. I felt as only wanting to be left alone and spend days, maybe weeks, feeling the silent vibrations of those walls. These rocks did not need me, I needed them. They belonged there as I also did. I felt as though they kept me on a straight line while present, afraid once we left, the tentacles of the outside world would again pull me sideways. So much beauty laid out in front of me. Why could life not be the same? I started wondering where did it all go wrong and how all here was so right? Present here, the other side of the coin where few reached, and even if they did, had they felt what I was feeling being so much what I always sought in deep contrast from the urban life. Away from the hot streets of steaming oils throughout the heat of the days, the air filled with smoke from the constant running machines, cars or otherwise, all allowing the masses to follow their daily patterns with the bells and whistles of clocks and their reminding alarms from cell phones and horns. Crawling through the portal led me to peace.

Riding through the cities always coerced me to the billboards planted up high toward the skies as to not miss the materialism they said should complement our lives. The needs present here in the now, all perfect again. Petroglyphs lasted centuries, the billboards will always be torn down to depict shinier, bigger and faster objects brainwashing so many minds with more "must haves" filled with desires. This "here", my choice and such a privilege to be among the remains of a culture still present even if having moved a bit further up the roads. We left at some point not having planned to stay overnight. My hunger had only been given a tiny morsel to taste. I promised myself to come back, well prepared for at least a week or maybe longer.

We did so well together that upon our return to his house decided to prepare ourselves for another adventure. Our destination would be Toroweap. The northern rim of the Grand Canyon where few went. Sixty miles of unpaved roads, its surface being of a silty soil called caliche, in which tires would only spin endlessly when wet. We needed a visit to Costco, a new experience as never been in such a store. From Whitney Pocket to Costco ended up being a culture shock. The volume of items amazed me, the variety endless. We shopped for items for their home and for some food I would prepare to take with us. We settled for potato and chicken pasta salads so we would not have to cook while in Toroweap. All went well, and the three of us left on a very early Friday morning. We read of bad weather in the forecast, but not until Sunday evening as we planned only a couple nights at one of the six very primitive campsites available. First come, first served. Less than 1,000 people per year visited that location of the rim, the odds with us. Two ways to approach the thought of such forecast which by then stored in the back of my mind, confronted us. The first would be, believing such forecast and being cautious, staying ahead of it by a few hours. Twelve being a good number. The wiser approach would be to postpone this ride for another time, as we both knew the road would be unforgiving if the rains made their presence. Not going to give up, of course, we would stay ahead of the weather. Try to. That little background voice of mine not powerful enough to hold us back.

A fine ride. We each rode our own. I would at times pass him while he photographed the scenery, at other times, he moved on while Spirit on a water break. A sign appeared "The Arizona strip, where the West stays wild". Sure enough, an old schoolhouse came into view. A structure originally built in 1922. A multipurpose dwelling used as a church, a town hall and a dance hall before the locals drifted away in the mid 60's. Arson destroyed it in 2000, but rebuilt and rededicated in October of 2001. A left took us up to Mount Trumbull. The steep grades of white caliche, still dormant that day, reached an elevation of 6,500 feet. After passing diverse land jurisdictions such as Bureau of Land Management, State land, National Monument, National Park and private land, we came to the gates of Toroweap, feeling as if we arrived at the gates of Heaven. Still no sign of the Grand Canyon though. The last couple miles turned rougher, and as the protruding rocks stared at me, we got stuck having taken a wrong line. Michael was nowhere in sight, probably already setting up camp, when a four wheel drive SUV showed up, passed us, stopped and towed us up. Nice save. We arrived at the primitive campground, and sure enough, Michael already set up, all ears listening to my rescue story. He said he would have come back within another hour. I thanked him for that. Nice shaded space with no need to set up our tent. Perfect weather to sleep under the stars. The bivy bag would be enough.

Even though we could have walked, we took the short ride to the rim and there, a 3,000 foot sheer cliff vertical drop with no guardrails. Just us and some fractured rocks seemingly barely balanced. Down below, the Colorado River silently flowing. Dramatic, it took my breath away and a bit too much to grasp all at the same time. Very quickly, I put Spirit on his leash, not being the time or place for him to roam around freely. I took him to his car not too long after as I wanted to deal with the camera and my own fear of heights.

Very carefully I must say, I walked the rim back and forth, sometimes jumping on those giant rocks so precariously balanced while I felt much admiration and a constant sense of my stomach floating down the river 3,000 feet below. One of those natural wonders a person could sit in front of without ever lifting their eyes, constantly finding a new ridge, a dry waterfall plainly visible, new colors, silhouettes. So hard to describe it all. A time one needs to experience as photos would never do justice. With three sources of light, the skies, the walls and the bottom of the canyon, hard to photograph. Sunset came along. A sunset in Toroweap. One to never miss as the canyon turned darker and the silhouettes of the ridges stood out in contrast with the golds and blues of the skies getting darker, a giant lid slowly covering it all throwing a darkness which would last until sunrise.

I did not sleep much that night. Even being at a distance from the rim, that hollow space had me floating and pulling me down throughout my dreams. On and off, eyes shut for a while, at other times staring at the stars so bright from a lack of any light pollution, I must have finally fallen asleep because I woke up just as sunrise started its show. A patch of blue skies, some cluttered clouds and the silhouette of a tree. My welcoming curtain rising for the day as I grabbed my camera to capture it all. It turned out to this day to be one of my favorite photos. Only one night instead of two, as Michael while looking at the skies, proposed we leave and not wait for the next day. Cut off from any connection, a premonition. I agreed and we packed not wanting to ignore such thoughts. Being too short of a stay, one more time, I promised myself we would be back. The rough couple miles of road now downhill, an easier task than when we arrived did not present any problems. Passing through those same gates crossed the day before, one of the arms of the sidecar snapped a bolt, the main one. I always carried so many spare parts. Not that one! A "Duh!" moment. Michael and I looked at each other a bit concerned. We dug through parts laying around the ranger's station as no one was on duty at the time, trying to borrow a nut and bolt from an antique grader parked in a field not too far away. All to no avail. This is when being in numbers came in handy, as he offered, truly without a choice, to ride the 60 miles to Colorado City, find a hardware store and come back. Nothing else to do but wait and savor being there while I knew he would enjoy his solo ride.

I had never been so happy seeing a trail of dust approaching on the road coming over the horizon feeling as in one of those adventure movies when the hero returns to save the day. I recognized the pattern of Michael's motorcycle headlights. He came back with the right nut and bolt in solid grade eight, even purchased a spare set, some food, water and a lunch to go. What a treat. Nothing to complain about considering our location. The repair did not take long, and once again we took off, deciding we would ride a bit more together, closer to each other. Another premonition. Sure enough, west of us and a day early, the clouds started to form. We decided to head straight towards Colorado City, east instead of west. The sooner we would get off the unpaved roads, the better it would be. Not long after, Michael parked on the side of the road with a flat tire. He carried plugs, but no compressor. I had one. We went to work after unloading all of his camping gear to put the bike on its center stand, and another repair behind us. By now, the concern of imminent rain was present more than ever, the clouds moving much faster than we thought. Barely another couple miles and one more flat tire. The same one. I noticed it being right behind him. We knew the drill. What would be the chance of having two punctures? That is exactly what we found out after wasting a bit of water to find the air bubbles. Once again all fixed up, this time we kept an even shorter distance between us as the sky continued getting darker by the minute. At that point in time, east or west did not matter. I could see no way out from the upcoming downpour. Sure enough, the drops materialized. Slow at first, but not long after, turning into buckets of water precisely directed at us. Watching his rear tire, he started to fishtail. Riding on wet caliche is like riding on ice. I came upon him quickly and signed him to stop. He refused, and only a few feet later he laid it down, bike and all. Caliche has that peculiar property to build up layers on a tire and in the wheel wells. It becomes mud against mud resulting in a total loss of traction. To make matters worse, it would only take a few more feet to lock up the wheels. He could not have picked a better spot right at a small intersection of a narrower farm road. We tried many times to pick up his bike, after again unloading his camping gear. With high morale, we started laughing at the fact that the only movement his bike agreed on was to slide down on its belly.

We eventually set the bike up straight on the side of the road while we pushed Old Faithful out of the way. Nothing else left to do but set our tents in the rain and on the mud while our boots built up inches of caliche under their soles. Set up about 50 feet from each other, we talked when the rain noise would lighten a bit. Well prepared and happy campers for those few nights spent on the side of the road, we ate, slept and read with ample water, food, and a book. My only concern was finishing it. I would have nothing left to read and would have to start it over. No one passed by those days, not a single soul even when the skies lightened up. We could only wait for the roads to dry. Michael built a little snowman made of mud and rested it on a fence pole. It would be our message to leave when it dried. By the third day, a ranger drove by and saw us. He stopped and opened his cooler, telling us to help ourselves to all the extra water and candy bars carried. He called Michael's wife with his SAT phone to give her our news, we had turned lemons into a nice sweet lemonade. Poor Spirit with nothing else to do but eat, sleep and briefly come out of the tent a few times a day to relieve himself. I never knew this dog of mine could sleep so much. I did not hear a single complaint.

By the fourth day, really enjoying being there, a four wheel drive truck passing by stopped and gave us more food. We hung our clothes to dry. Our little caliche weatherman, as we called it, dried up nicely, and we decided with a bit of sadness to start heading back. With magnificent skies ahead of us, a few clouds present flying by, the sun felt good, and besides a few patches of wet roads which we sped through, a perfect ride. We came out of the mud, the paved road welcoming and with sticks in hand cleaned up the wheel wells, the tires, anything caliche stuck on. If left there, all would soon turn into hard rock. Our knowledge and experience of the outdoors paid off. One of the main aspects being to never leave camp thinking we would get back to civilization in a normal amount of time and ever fighting or complaining against Mother Nature, as it would not have been of any use. We took those days as they came with the best humor and enjoyment possible, never at risk or in any danger, building up memories we would carry with us for years to come.

Back north of St. George, the map stared at me once again, states foreign to us being dreamed of. Lander, Wyoming, the town where KC and Mia lived, friends met in Utah. Outdoor enthusiasts themselves, they knew, as we call them, all "the good spots". We headed that way and while almost there, stopped at Red Rock Canyon first where the landscape from far away showed us its luscious greens and flowers of all colors blooming with red sandstone trim laid out circling it so perfectly.

My faithful companions, Mother Nature and Spirit, so much thinking of them as the greatest gifts I could have ever received. As incomplete my thoughts were about life in years past, I started feeling the opposite with an easier acceptance being a matter of choice, balance and path taken I did not want or allow myself to abandon. Friends traveled with us even if having never met them, ones who held us up as we also held them up in their own passage as though we started this circle of life and enclosed all these questions which did not have answers, realizing too well, that such circle would never close. Once a narrow path, thoughts became wide avenues which I tried to keep uncluttered as much as possible.

Good times being around KC and Mia. The start of a true friendship which would develop over the years as fortunately it sometimes happens.

Pizza night, roaming in the quaint little town of Lander, a drive in their four wheeler up the mountains to show us the town from above and many conversations took up the times spent. Spirit made himself at home. Nothing could have been any better. With map laid out on the table we planned, for a change, to move on somewhere a bit more north between Yellowstone and the Grand Tetons. It sounded all good in spite of the promise of mosquitoes making their home in those areas.

We left on an early morning towards Grassy Lake Road, a mile or so south of the entrance to Yellowstone enticed by the description of primitive campsites right along the Snake River. July would be a bad month to adventure into crowded National Parks, but this space remained off the grid, besides warnings of much road construction while getting there. We detoured through Riverton for some shopping at Walmart. Food and mosquito spray which would not contain any DEET. A few hours later, we found our destination. A paved road which quickly turned into an unpaved one, and every quarter mile or so on our left, campsites laid out right on the river. Perfect locations and outstanding views where we could easily use up the 14 day limit. It turned out to be more like 14 seconds. I settled on one of the campsites a bit more isolated. As I got off the bike, Spirit still in his car, I did not even have the chance or the willingness to remove my full face helmet and gloves. Thousands of mosquitoes swarmed around us forming moving shadows while diving on Spirit. I heard his cries and saw a look in his eyes never seen before. Without even thinking if this was going to work out or not I started the engine, and sadly enough we headed back to the main road. What to do now? Where to go? One of those bumps in the road. Totally disappointed as anywhere else would be filled wall to wall with tourists, I started feeling like a whining spoiled kid forgetting to put it all in perspective. I should not easily forget the good fortune of us being on the road with an unparalleled freedom. Sometimes we could not have it all. Such bumps would appear and we would just have to blend in or go around them.

We ended up riding the roads of Yellowstone Park and stopped to watch Old Faithful erupt. We and hundreds more. It turned out to be interesting being in the midst of so many people. Parents and their children, hundreds of cameras taking the same photos as I also did. Yellowstone is a beautiful park with its roads basically forming a figure eight. We needed to find shelter for the night. The campgrounds full, we headed in the direction of Cody. It made for a long riding day from Lander. An odd looking dwelling appeared on a hill to the right of us looking like a haunted house, black with unfinished wings from all sides which I took a few photos of. I would have liked to get closer but a sign was there. "No Trespassing ~ The Smith Mansion". About a hundred feet away I noticed an RV park welcoming tent campers, and even though it looked full, I gave it a try as the day was getting very late and both tired. It turned out to not be a problem. A large grassy area, the owner dog friendly, wifi and a nightly bonfire for everyone who camped there. Not exactly what I looked for, but the mosquitoes only a few. The present comfort of showers, comfortable grounds, the town of Cody nearby taking away the worry of provisions, all nicely surfaced. One night led to a few more, thinking of it as a new base camp with many daily rides all surrounding us. Chief Joseph Highway and Bear's Tooth Pass, the main attractions. I remembered riding them many years ago while on two wheels, but forgotten the beautiful roads carved through very tall and rugged mountains, tight hairpin turns and pull outs which allowed us to be in the middle of wide panoramas with a valley down below. We made it to Red Lodge, another quaint and touristic little town. One which served a great cheeseburger at the Red Box Car. I treated myself. We stayed cool throughout July and my admiration for the country's geography increasing by the day, especially after riding Bear's Tooth Pass a couple times. Whose idea was it to defy the elements and build such a dramatic road? One at the highest elevation of any highway in the Northern Rockies. Even in mid-summer the snow banks reached ten feet high, a closed road during winter times. Some days we just vegetated. Some nothing days lingering with the speed of the sun going by. Much reading, playing with Spirit, a nice nap around noon, a couple good meals while developing my "one-pan" cooking.

Photography turned into a serious hobby as a sponsor offered us a couple nice cameras and lenses. It became so uplifting to hunt throughout the day for those sights that would create vivid memories. I learned if one really looked, the most eccentric images were the common ones. So many, at times including myself, took their surroundings too often for granted and overlooked. As we sat within the look outs, the winds became new music to my ears. Dead calm or at times without warning, like a freight train they would burst out loud and clear, moving in waves the tips of all the trees nearby. With the strangest correlation, Mother Nature taught me the lessons of life while reading many books becoming my tutors. I remembered when not long ago I would say to myself "Shouldn't the world stop turning now? Don't they know what happened to me?" I believed for the longest time being the only victim on earth. Those days, I read and understood another phrase "Do I wither up and disappear, or do I make the best of my time left?" The difference of thoughts between then and now such an unimaginable forward momentum. I began reading *"Tuesdays with Morrie"* which affected me in a good way. In the book, Morrie, while slowly dying, decided to share his thoughts and memories every Tuesday with a writer. His life went on *"one precious day at the time"*. I focused on those precious days. With no avoidance for his death he said *"Learn how to die and you will learn how to live"*. I did not ever want to go through my own life half asleep and on auto-pilot. The influence of the pages intensely renewed my energy towards the journey and brought me closer to the truth.

We moved on towards Bozeman where I felt urbanized. I liked that little town and looked for shade on Main Street as I wanted to stroll. Friendly crowd, cozy atmosphere, fond of dogs, sidewalk cafes and taco stands. Much chatting. Of course the chatting a lot to do with a dog wearing goggles and riding in a sidecar. From day one, back in Dahlonega, that aspect never changed. We could come back to all of this any day as we camped by Fairy Lake, a bit north of Bozeman having the best of both worlds for a while. Fairy Lake Road needed high clearance, yet not too bad for us if taken at a slow pace. We roamed the area looking for dead wood to cook with, took many photos and hiked a bit here and there. Those days spent were of more magic served so graciously. Nice blue skies, a few clouds passing by and bringing on a resemblance of coolness, while the landscape, including wild flowers of all colors, was what postcards were made of. I stayed up late many nights watching my fire dance, always mesmerized by the flames. It meant getting up later the next day, sometimes too lazy to go anywhere.

I want to write "Man living in his sheepherder wagon and his five horses, full time on the road for 26 years, meets beautiful woman in Montana and together they live happily ever after". That is the story. It would be more a headliner than anything else as there is much more to it. I met Ron Dakota one evening while returning to Fairy Lake. A red sheepherder's wagon with a white roof parked on the side of the road, five horses grazing contained by an electric fence. How could I have not made a U-turn to check it out. He must have heard Old Faithful, as this man opened the door and welcomed us to his "Americana", as he called it. Sixty-eight years old, of average stature, graying hair, his insight totally and immediately overcame me. He and his horses rode six days a week, 20 miles per day, often on roads which did not have guard rails and all the while needing much grass every night for his buddies. He trailered a smaller wagon for his tools and much water as each horse drank ten gallons per day. I felt lucky to be with Spirit, so much less maintenance. Too many questions and getting late, we decided to come back the next day to spend more time together, maybe fix a meal. At 20 miles a day, I knew I would find him easily.

And we did the next day as he headed towards Ennis, Montana. In such amazement of his own life, I called it the simple life at first, only later realizing the chores of his daily maintenance. I then called it the "nice hard life"! Six wheels, 20 legs, three miles per hour, 50 gallons of water per day and two and a half tons of feed per month. I had found a kindred spirit, both curious about each other's journey. We did not quite have the same thinking, but there existed a common denominator called "the passion for the road". We came back with some provisions, my camp stove, a pan and cooked a nice dinner filled with interesting conversations. We decided we would again meet in Ennis shortly. He did have a phone, the technology having not escaped him. Couple days later, a kind lady in Ennis and owner of the "Rusty Cowboy Gallery", Teri Freeman, seeing him passing through town offered her pasture, herself owning a couple horses. I got in touch with her and she also offered us a space for our tent. All so promising towards a new adventure and the many experiences awaiting from new people met. We settled in Ennis, right behind the Gallery and her couple barns. Kind Ron full of stories, Teri, herself a generous woman and well traveled, Spirit by my side, dinner that night ran late and we found ourselves as three kids who had not seen each other for ages with too many stories to tell. Too busy talking, I failed miserably while cooking. There were no complaints, yet no praises either. It satisfied our hunger. The main and most important aspect, as then on we each sat back comfortably in the body conforming chairs filled with pillows in Teri's house, and life's discussions continued.

Ron's definition of our society, culture and present civilization awakened some questions all evening. According to him, we still attended kindergarten. I could not argue much with that definition as the doors of my own school always stayed open having never stopped enriching myself with a luxury called time. Ron's own journey penetrated my bottomless desire to cultivate my soul even further. During the evening, which lasted late into the night, I felt as sitting outside a circle drawn by those two. Present, a spark between them in their words exchanged, certain looks, almost a defiance. The cowgirl and the cowboy both strong headed. An image obvious to me started taking shape even if not yet to them. A date night for those two a few days later did not take long to happen. The rest of the story? Well, it is history. They were meant to be together, love took over as they sailed on with much respect for each other. Today, they both live in Bandera, Texas. Horses, wagon, chickens. They all have moved to a warmer climate and Ron is now on a different road, the one of happiness with a companion in his life.

One at a time my own companions lined up stronger than ever. Spirit my human, as I called him, Mother Nature with whom I kept a tight close knit relationship, friends surfacing through our journal while following us, my Mother always present through a telephone. All had truly become "The Oasis of my Soul".

> "Any change, any loss, does not make us victims. Others can shake you, surprise you, disappoint you, but they cannot prevent you from acting, from taking the situation you're presented with and moving on. No matter where you are in life, no matter what your situation, you can always do something. You always have a choice and the choice can be power" [Blaine Lee]

We often lived, as I like to believe, isolated, detached and off the beaten track from society. Often times when staring at the horizon which calmly settled my mind, questions and apprehension filled me with no replies that could ever satisfy me. I never plunged into politics, deep rooted religion, sexuality, violence or confrontations. Only considerate discussions. I never used profanities, yet I was blunt saying my peace as it should be with never an intention of harming my neighbor. I voiced my own outlook of my thoughts with the hope that it would be received with respect as I respected others. I wrote the hypothesis of my sentiments because I read of others deeply. They construed so many agendas that maybe the reality of their own words hid in contrast with mine which I took pleasure in showing, making them understand their full values in contradiction with games sadly played instead. So often I felt let down by the flow of others, submerged and sinking deep in their superficial pathways of life sometimes never seeming quite real. A bit like floating in space without touching the core that would make us who we should be. I silently often said "wake up". Lift only your arms to hug and not to harm. Soften your vision to embrace one another and not glare as if one was your enemy. Instead feel as he or she is a loved one.

Social media started to leave an imprint on me. I became permeated from the novelty. The Internet pages brought in new discoveries, open doors toward other's lives. Same doors allowing more views into our own lives. Commercialism knocked on our door. Writing for magazines, attending rallies to demonstrate my "one-pan" cooking, interviews, even a television appearance or two. My intent was always to share the beauty which surrounded us. Yet, a trace of ego surfaced. Our names in magazines? Many attending our classes? Listening to us on the radio or watching us on television? I did in its beginnings, enjoy it. I thought with much honesty everyone surrounding us planted the same seeds called "sharing" and "friendship", none stripping away the comfort of my soul regained slowly over the past years, the forcefulness of such a circle of society not unpleasant. My own steps to climb always staring at me, obstacles and hurdles absent, we went with the flow. Sometimes I felt expressing my own space so strongly maybe inflated or just a caricature of life I wanted to see and feel overestimating its therapeutic powers. Contrary to those beliefs, my personal expressions I shared as such contained the present reality.

None of it pulled us away from Montana for the time being. We stayed in Ennis exploring the area. The gold-mining towns of Pony, Sterling, Virginia City and rode a few times over a favorite road called Gravelly Range Road. I called it "the road to nowhere", even if 70 miles of it going through bear country connected Ennis to the Centennial Valley with spectacular views across a massive open plateau. It is one of the most scenic routes in Montana. When asked why I like that road so much, I never quite come up with a reply, only saying one had to experience it themselves. A windy unpaved road in good condition which did not seem to have an end to it. Right past a slight peak one day, I saw a sheepherder wagon. Another one. No horses this time, but four dogs. A young man came out of the door and signaled me to come over, already wondering what would anyone be doing at such altitude, especially without horses. His name was Bigne and he called his dogs "dog". Every single one of them. We immediately developed a language barrier, as Bigne lived in Peru, could barely understand English and my Spanish is about as poor as it could be. Him dumbfounded by Spirit wearing his goggles and helmet is an understatement. A bond formed right away. He loved it up there and he turned out to be a sheepherder working for a rancher. The sheep grazed a few hills away, a couple thousand head and the dogs would bring them back. In no time, invited, I sat in his wagon. Mi casa is su casa, I understood that right away. A comfy bench, a one burner cook stove, and lunch appeared. Rice with chicken, carrots and beans. A full plate and I could only compliment his generosity with the few bananas and peanut butter I carried along for the day. All so delicious as the experience spiced it up. We talked much, we managed to communicate, Spanish not being too different from French, my maternal language. We spoke about life, this nature we both felt at home within and his family. His Boss, as he called him, would come by once or twice a week and drop off food, water, anything else he needed and a fully charged battery. The weather being cold enough, he did not need refrigeration. We knew the drill. We lived alike. He owned a cell phone which only worked a quarter of a mile away and to my surprise, a DVD player for some great Peruvian music videos he played for me. Photos of his family pinned all over the back wall, he showed me who was who and at times his heavy silence and look in his eyes told me how much he missed them for the three months he spent working on those hills. Upon leaving, I told him I would be back to see him soon. I asked him what I could bring. "Nada" he said, "just your friendship". We went back a few days later. For some odd reason I took him some donuts! I figured, why not? Maybe they did not have donuts in Peru. Fresh donuts right out of the fryer from Ennis. A luxury I could, health-wise, only afford a couple times a year. He liked them and made us some coffee to go along. Hard days to forget as I often wondered if he came back for another season. Maybe I will find out some day when we return.

I would often look at Spirit, meaning really observing him, feeling his own soul through his eyes and body movements. Abused in his first year, I would still at times, sadly enough, see his tail between his legs. It would not last long, as when locking eyes or hearing my voice, he would realize it was then as today is now, and if anyone could live the present, he could and did. It shocked many when I would say I learned a lot from him. He did not have the ability to make the choices encumbering my own life, content and happy with his own times living as we did. He did not have to make decisions as I did, which through my own awareness became harder as my thoughts of the consequences of the consequences only kept increasing. Like him, quite often, I would have to let go. One really never knew what would be around the corner from a judgment taken or about to take and could lose their daily freedom doing so, tilting the delicate balance. One I always tried to maintain.

Ron had already left on his way to the VA hospital for a yearly check up and we had to go. I knew somehow he would return. They would be back together. September again, soon. More anniversaries, birthday, holidays, all coming up. We headed east after some long good byes and many words of wisdom. Time to get back on paved roads before Old Faithful would start screaming from too much pain while bouncing on the recent unpaved paths. With a general idea of its location, we rode to Bannack. A few pit stops, stretching, water breaks, plain old breathing. Back on Highway 287 from Ennis we once again went through Virginia City crowded as ever, Sheridan, Twin Bridges where we headed southeast on Highway 41. A longer stop in Dillon. I found myself being squeezed between two centuries when a beautiful structure caught my attention. The Hotel Melten build in 1897, while across the street, as defiant as possible, recently painted graffiti on the walls of an abandoned warehouse. How ironic it would be the sight the guests would see from their windows. Off the beaten path, we made it to Bannack where we found some campsites. Unlike Virginia City, no fire trucks loaded with 82 tourists, each at $8 a head as driving in Bannack prohibited. A very quiet and well preserved State Park, we could blend in with an atmosphere of years past when gold mining was in its heydays. Since the first nugget found in the gravel of nearby Grasshopper Creek, the town touched the lives of many. At one time, the population over 3,000 remained full and vibrant. Like many gold mining towns, the mines dried up and everyone left for greener pastures. Everything remained well preserved and the buildings became open to the public. The school, the saloon, the city hall, a court house, private homes, the blacksmith, all a photographer's delight with so many pages of historical facts.

More comments on our journal came in by the day. One always stuck with me. "You are living the Dream". With a capital D. I appreciated it all being a dream promised to live. Most did not know why we chose the road as no reason to explain unless specifically asked. We did not have any regrets for this therapy of ours. A choice versus the harsh reality of medication, counseling, the "do so…", "say so…" and words I unfortunately read, heard and not well received, such as "get over it". I felt the other world, the one on the other side never too far being a harsh one. The choice was a promise which ended up including scraping funds day to day, scrounging for our needs at times, but never disturbed by it all as my wealth came from within. Our richness did not consist in the extent of our possessions, but in the fewness of our wants. I met a man who lost his son 13 years earlier as I found out being part of a conversation. During a moment of silence as my heart felt his own pain, I asked him, hesitating, *Do you still think about him every day?* All this while trying to keep my composure. With glassy eyes he replied in a trembling voice *"every day, every day…"*. A man also in constant forward mobility on a path close to ours, his own therapy. He climbed Mount Everest, gone horseback riding through Southern and Northern Africa and a member of a mountain rescue team in Scotland where he resided. I met him while horseback riding off the beaten path from Wyoming to Montana. *"You go on"*, he said, *"the good days start outweighing the bad days as time goes on, even if the frustration of those dead end mind sets keep visiting the past moments, present and future"*.

I read another comment one day *"Ara, your photography is simply awesome. However my friend, your commentary is a bit too abstract, too deep and is contradictory to the beauty of your photos. Neither do justice to each other…"*. I grimaced when I read those words finding a certain reality to their meaning and represented the opinion of many who would have preferred brighter spoken words on my pages, a better entertainment value, maybe an in-depth ride report which by then the fashion and a dime a dozen. Such were never my goals. I felt my awareness with particular brightness to it and not a numbness as peaks and valleys are present in everyone's lives. My pages written, my life lived so freely, none meant to hide in those valleys and peek out only when on the summits. Reality encompassed the complete array of life, the eternal balance and without one scale, such balance would always be tipped. I write for myself so often reading back my own words discovering over and over where that day's mile marker was. In the words of *Dr. Seuss* *"Be who you are and say what you feel because those who mind don't matter and those who matter don't mind"*.

The MT initials of Montana remained. Wandering continued more than ever as I knew soon we would have to drop south, the seasons changing. Having passed Broadus once without stopping, we backtracked after reading more about the little town with hidden treasures. Its heart was indeed beating strongly, especially with a sign stating "World's best milkshake". An inviting sugar rush right around the corner. I saw a rare bowling alley, unfortunately closed. I met by chance the owner/operator/bottle washer/ theater/gym/pool resort next door. Seeing this man take a garbage can out to the sidewalk when the sign said "Closed", I guessed right he would be the owner. Doug, a music teacher from Seattle, willing to give me a personal tour of his dwelling which contained all of the above. We started with the small city theater, its stage being the gym when not showing movies, which I thought clever. Everyone in town when buying a new sofa donated their old ones to him, including a dentist chair and the rear seat of an old Oldsmobile. The pizzas baked near the entrance, one could eat and watch a movie at the same time. In a dentist chair! We talked about the big city where he could easily have stayed with a larger paycheck, as well as a much higher stress level. A young lady came by while chatting and applied for a job. He told her to come back in a couple days to start training. She wondered about a job application, to which he replied, there was none here. Life might not be easy, but we keep it simple, he said. We stepped into the resort simply laid out in the backyard with a huge round pool, wood decks, floating lounges and from Walmart, shower curtains of all colors with palm tree designs on the surrounding walls for affect. Hanging, a big "Welcome" sign for everyone in town. I let him continue his tasks, found some shade across the street for Spirit, and time came to try the "they said" best Dairy Queen in the world. It turned out to be located in an antique store selling a bit of everything. One large family sitting in a corner took up half the store, locals we chatted with as they let me take their photo. I picked raspberry as my flavor. I finished it with no clue if the best in the world as not being raised with milk shakes, but I found it to be delicious, followed by a shot of espresso to counteract the sugar slump slowly coming on.

Being connected to the Internet started to feel like a double edged sword. I still could not understand the ill content of a few more nasty e-mails received. Again, they troubled me as I am always inclined to believe in the goodness of others which we often experienced. At such times, I felt bursting from a thorn which deflated all the common knowledge acquired from past years. I tried to comprehend what made the core of one staying silent through whispers, only to one day become loud and destructive with many insinuations and innuendos, our world not being a fake stage. I slowly detached myself further keeping a greater distance. We lived in our own world which I found to be better than most, one of vast plains, empty spaces, higher plateaus with no footprints. Much did not make sense when the hurt passed. I found ourselves better off being free, able to think, going through our own emotions and taking the appropriate steps moving forward. We stayed true to the shiny path, avoiding the shoulders of obscurity some decided to cloud us with.

We rode through the Badlands arriving at the Devil's Tower, passing through the town of Scenic, population ten. Back in Wyoming, Devil's Tower a surprise, as one rides up and down some hills, a flat plateau following, and unanticipated, this "thing" protruded out of the ground. A striped rock formation rising 1,200 feet. No one has agreed yet how it all came about. There are many possible interpretations. Volcanic or erosion? Some think the tower formed half a mile underground millions of years ago. I would not find out, only admire it and watch the few people climbing to its summit. The days started shortening as September approached with cooler nights. I often used my sleeping bag liner and Spirit slept with his coat on.

We went back to the little town of Scenic which I found by making a wrong turn. Lucky us. A few buildings on each side of Main Street and a small fuel station with only regular available where I topped off our tank. It doubled as the local store with its shelves mostly bare, only stocked with the necessities. Few photos on the walls, all dating early 1900's, not much more information, none as much as the lady at the counter. She must have been lonely as she started chatting about the history of the town, past and present. She pointed towards the bar and told about the jail next to it and of another behind the store. Not much ever going on, except during the Sturgis motorcycle rally nearby. Parking space would then be scarce by the bar, the main attraction which that day remained closed. Called the Longhorn Saloon, at one time featured in National Geographic as in the past, exchange of bullets was not uncommon. It turned out the lady and her grandmother owned most of this little town of ten. Much room for camping nearby, but no rental vacancies available, left empty due to the increased indoor drug activities. Without any law enforcement, the only solution for them. This would have been indeed the ultimate hide out. Not much changed from a century ago, including the jails which were fully functional if needed. I went in. My first and last jail time on our journey. It ended our stay in Scenic with no one else to talk to. No one parked next to us, not even another dog prowling the streets. About 1,000 miles away, The Oasis waited for our third winter season visit.

Many miles, overnights, photos, always "Americana" while avoiding the freeways. From the statue of a Native American Indian holding his torch of hope towards the sun, fields of sunflowers on their own daily twists and turns, old rusty cars with much back seat room, black giant rubber cylinders wishing they were our tires, older and newer fuel stations with always the same prices and creative murals in those unheard little towns, so much more. We experienced it all while dropping south.

Alpine, Texas. Only 58 miles from The Oasis. We booked a motel room while a deluge of rain made me question if our road would be passable. Six months had gone by and both ready to enjoy our land and its surroundings. I knew every season we came back would be different. Trying to not think about it and riding with the flow we arrived the next day within that silent always welcoming space. All was the same but different. For the first time I called it "Home". How could I not? As *Robert Frost* had written *"The City has withdrawn into itself and left at last the country to be the country"*.

The balancing act of the nights and days required a new scale. Absent more than ever the calendar and clock. Some tasks needed to be taken care of, not many, with all the time in the world. We stayed in for days watching the skies and nibbling at the plate Mother Nature served us. Not a single portion I could resist. The shapes drawn above from winds as giant hands rearranging them never leaving the canvas still. Happy times and many photos shared with friends. Some of whom we met in person, some only over the Internet and through phone calls. As October 13th once again rolled around, the most important person I wanted to share it all with remained physically absent. One more quiet birthday celebration mixed with emotions. My Mother and I talked for a long time that day. Dreams took place played by the incessant memories. My own dreams, never expecting anyone to understand them. The more beautiful and serene my surroundings became, the more I bowed to Lance's sacrifice allowing me to be on such a path. Experiencing so much artistry and refinements these past three years, the boundaries of the dreams and reality had started to blend in. Spirit, happy to be back, regained his own complete and unobstructed freedom. Showing off, he would run in circles 100 miles per hour. Nothing had moved or disappeared. My Center of the Universe, those fire rings surrounded by beautiful rocks and pecan wood benches, a pile of firewood, all intact as I started cooking stews at the time. A pot hanging over the fire, easy and comfort food enough for a couple days as I watched the flames and the smoke dancing with each other.

Sunrises and sunsets became part of the only true realities. With always front row seats they marked the day starting, the nights ending and vice versa. The shows lasted a long time. We went on to Terlingua a few days later. I forced myself to leave The Oasis. As usual, it turned out to be a whole day affair, pure entertainment of the mind and more. We were back here a bit too early, as the temperatures hovered around 100. I felt as being in one of those western movies, the spaghetti kind with the hot wind blowing heavy layers of dust, a twister here and there and the sun brighter than the flash grandpa used with his camera. Shade could have brought in many dollars in rental if ever any found. Riding through town, it must have been siesta time as being the only vehicle out and about, all the stores closed, including the bank and the post office. This is when and where "my" and "self" could easily cohabitate. We did for the months to come.

Different weather patterns this time around. It rained in the evenings bringing on a welcomed cool breeze as one day the thermometer reached a high of 119. Profound thunder would scream from a not so typical rainy sky. The sun, as behind a rising curtain, would try to make an appearance giving the storms a peculiar orange cast. The power of it all so intense, and yet, I would feel a certain friendliness. Electricity present in the air, I tasted the coppery smell mixed with the scent of wet earth. The Oasis had never welcomed us in such a fashion.

Eventually, the storms did pass leaving behind good weather as in past years with plenty of water filling our loaned cistern. Social events started to take place all around us discovering them through a local weekly one page newspaper. They took place in Terlingua, Alpine, Marathon, Fort Davis, Marfa and even in Valentine. Mostly on the weekends with big crowds from Austin, Houston, Dallas and even further. They would come in for a taste of this original West. Much music, most of it free, open art galleries and the Mustang Shelby cars forming a rally came in as they did every year. Any occasion and excuse good for a gathering. Such as the "wig day" and the "stupid race", when most would dress up and with beer can in hand walk a couple miles. Bicycle races took place, a marathon, some legit, others called as such because it sounded good, appealing, contradictory and humorous. In Terlingua, the Day of the Dead celebration came around. Marfa had their own Cat Woman. A lady with a black jumpsuit from head to toe laying and purring on the sidewalks. Alpine, its Art Walk with hundreds of people attending and art car parades. The area stood out on the map of many with eventually endless events going on at all times. Fortunately, miles away from it all, we could choose when and where to go. We attended quite a few of the events, camera in hand, taking many photos and shooting some videos.

Jackson Brown Jr. had written *"Sometimes the heart sees what is invisible to the eye"*. Could the eye sometimes meet the heart? I assured myself it did. A reader of our journal approached us one day commenting *"Great entry this time around Ara, it was not just about you"*. He lived in the area full time and I only smiled, sadly I must say. Obvious, his eyes never met his heart, his path leading to each other closed while not seeing life in its present reality as I did, always confronting it. Honesty is the core, constantly finding few could handle that notion of the space they navigated in, trying too hard to customize it to their own terrain. I sometimes tried to explain why I wrote my journal. The fact that it was mine and mine only, never designed for entertainment purposes but as a sounding board, a companion throughout the journey trying to keep the flames going. They danced with the winds, extinguished with the rains, bright, dim and all in between, sometimes black as their leap smothered from a veil dropping when in the valleys of the mind. I could not go through life bottled up without filling pages of my own two way conversations. On Lance's birthday, his presents were wrapped with the multicolor bows surrounding me always undeterred from it all. The ribbons rearranged as I liked them, to look good when the day came for their unraveling. I waited that day as I always did and hoped. What else could I do? *"Life is just a mirror, and what you see out there, you must first see inside of you"*. [Wally Amos]

Winter gently marched on. As usual many rides through Big Bend National Park. We camped a few days at the State Park. Visited the papercrete dwellings in Marathon. More of Marfa with its food truck and pizza joint. Fort Davis. Our favorite ride on River Road to Presidio with a stop at the bakery. Someone gave me a kite providing me with new smiles as I flew it daily. We visited the Mosasaur Museum and made a video of it which I gifted. Many round trips to the nearby what we call "the swimming hole", a space filled with beautifully eroded rocks polished from two creeks joining together. We went to Houston for a few days visiting friends. Many local less traveled roads around Christmas and New Year, times which passed quietly. Chinati Hot Springs again. Yes, all the same and yet so different seeing and feeling once more or a few more times. I received some kind words while getting ready to leave *"I honor your commitment to exploring the mysteries of the outer world while searching the inner reaches of the inner experiences as well"*. How thoughtful and timely, as now, early April, 2010, all packed en route towards our fourth year north. On our last night, the moon rose around midnight. Shy at first, her face slightly draped by a distant unseen cloud, without a stumble, she then emerged slowly projecting her shadow into mine within this silent space quieter than the world on mute. A shooting star drawing its own trace above me went on to its next destination. Enchanted night, a final show at The Oasis for this time around. Morning came and we left. As in previous times, we stopped on top of the hill, looked back and waved our good byes.

Time did not stand still too long before we headed towards Bisbee, Arizona. Without a clue, we just did. I thought it had been a strange winter. "Different" was the key word. Not strange. The adventures more mental with much reading of various books filled with words which reverberated all along forming me into a mold a bit different than the previous ones. A mold more inquisitive toward the now and my surroundings. *William Least Heat-Moon* had written in his wonderful book *"Blue Highways"*: *"The old Jerseyman got up. At the door, he looked again at my license plate. 'The ancient Incas', he said, 'when they traveled the great mountain empire, were required to wear their own distinct costume so they could be recognized. What do we have now? A license plate? Ideas are a man's costume, his colors'"*.

On our way west, a true reality surfaced and took hold of me. Written by my good friend, *Tyler*: *"Don't fear your darkness because fear lets it win. Accept the bad but then let it go and focus on the good. We all have that gift in life and the ability to change ourselves, adapt, overcome and grow"*. It renewed my skills and challenged me for more adventures with much inner wealth present. Within a short time, we fell back into our familiar lifestyle while heading towards El Paso. With good weather and a strong tail wind I searched for the southern route, that hub always confusing me. Highway 178, which turned into Highway 136, called Columbus Road and also designated A003. All the same road, I never quite understood why. I guess I did not need to understand, only ride it. A bit further, that same road changed designation one more time. Before we arrived in Columbus, it became Highway 9. Passing the last little town of Animas, we made a left on Highway 80 towards Douglas, familiar surroundings from previous rides. Colorful Bisbee welcomed us quickly with easy camping at the Silverado Ranch, a few miles before town.

Why Bisbee? Much wondering while I knew too well of our plans, so unlike us, made to head up to Page, Arizona, and meet a group of overlanders on their way down to Overland Expo taking place in Amado of the same state. A big gathering of adventurers and their vehicles, movies, classes. It would be the first time we attended such a get together. We strolled around town, we rode the narrow streets up and down the hills, visited some galleries and the many stores filled with mementos designed for the tourists present. We stopped in front of a few buildings adorned with murals, some forming statues protruding on top of doorways. It felt like being back in the 60's. Quaint and crowded. I started questioning my decision heading north to meet this group and riding back down with them. An extra 1,000 miles with others I barely knew while we had been alone on this road for these few years. We did it anyhow. Something new. Maybe I would learn more aspects about the outdoors. So many maybes. Without a lot of choices to get to Page, much to my dislike, we rode freeways most of the way.

The group was nowhere to be seen when we arrived, them coming from Escalante. I checked on the condition of the road they planned to drive, one never maintained. The information from the rangers said the road at that time not being passable. I reached the group with a phone call, passing them the report. They did not agree and decided to try it. I followed them on their own GPS tracker, and sure enough, they made a U-turn to backtrack and take the easier and passable road. Reason for their tardiness. We finally hooked up a day late. One familiar face, all others strangers, all true off road vehicles as I felt out of place. Their leader in touch with me in past weeks had asked if I would be willing to be their chef for dinners and maybe breakfasts. We agreed, until another chef came into the picture emphasizing his specialty was to be "green", the expedition being called "the carbon neutral expedition" and I stepped down from the task truly relieved. We took a westerly direction towards the land south of the Grand Canyon having acquired permits to camp on them. We hit a network of roads all going in a multitude of directions getting lost many times which I could not quite understand why. Everyone did have maps and GPS available. I could hear "let's try this one... or that one..." mostly followed by U-turns. Some of those roads turned out to be too challenging for us. I often needed someone to stand on the step of the sidecar with Spirit so we would not roll over. The day became very frustrating even if the scenery remained fascinating, especially when we finally arrived, very late, by the rim of the Grand Canyon.

As quickly as the chef started cooking, he became drunk beyond limits. So did many. I sat nearby and just watched. With no idea of his doings, he would scream out loud what he threw in the big pot and none of it made any sense. It turned out his idea of going "green", which apparently seemed the latest thing on how to fit within any adventure social media group, was to use green garbage bags, green dishwashing liquid, green utensils. I found it hysterical and not the only one thinking so.

Dinner ended up being indescribable, simply indefinable. My peanut butter and jelly came in very handy. I lost my freedom the next day. So many stops I wanted to make and take photos or "just be" as when seeing wild horses run away passing us. Never again I thought.

Our first go around at Overland Expo in contrast turned into an incredible time. So many names who knew us and vice versa, faces I could place. Many vehicles of all sizes, all designed to go and get lost in the wilderness if only one could afford them. Outdoor gadgets galore from vendors under tents of all colors. Even the flags felt alive from a nice breeze blowing. Entertaining movies, great food, especially the banquet on Sunday evening. I skipped the cocktail parties as I do not drink, and sought some quiet times with my buddy by our campsite. Spirit always the main attraction, the riding dog, so sweet and friendly with everyone, only wanting to rub his head against their legs or be scratched on his behind. I think everyone took a picture of him. The only dog with his own name tag. Times were good. I could not wish I had made another decision in regards to the past 1,000 miles. Such remained behind us. We needed to move on. Which we did. Before we left, the organizer asked me if I would, for the next year's event, be willing to teach my "one-pan" cooking. I had some time to think about it, especially its logistics.

Fourth year on the road, another summer approaching. Not doing as well with heat, it became time to head further north and find some elevation. The green pastures of Colorado seemed inviting. The vibes felt good choosing such a destination, a vague one into the vast area it covered on the map. Entering the state, it was as the boundaries were marked. So pronounced, so much the other side of the coin from the red rocks of Arizona and Utah, as if Mother Nature decided to leave it all in its raw state, right at the border where the sign said "Welcome to Colorado". We came in through Durango on Highway 550 which would turn into what they call "The Million Dollar Highway". I am sure it would cost much more to build today. We passed Trimble, Hermosa, Tacoma, all in the heart of the San Juan National Forest and on our right, Electra Lake appeared blue and calm as ever. Silverton, and finally with few guard rails, the much talked about road started. Curve after curve it gave me ibby jibes with no shoulders as the width of the road stopped at the white lane. Sometimes no such white lanes. Looking down, trying hard not to. It did not seem to bother Spirit. After a mental and physical work out we arrived in Ouray. In that town stood an Oasis for some friends met at Big Bend National Park while themselves on the road. Throughout their own journey, they felt the need for a home. We had been trying to get together these past years. That time finally arrived and they welcomed us with open arms. Not having experienced the area, for that matter the heart of Colorado, I never stopped reading their own website. It was as if they hadn't ever left the path of being on the road in the middle of a geographical circle rich with many wonders of nature easily reachable. Lucky us, we had the complete upstairs to ourselves. Such true luxury.

They took us around in their 4 × 4 high clearance truck on roads we would have never reached, the scenes one by one trickling within the enormity of the present dimensions. It took a few days for the reel to slow down realizing right around us present spaces could fill a lifetime of adventures, their choice of a home perfect. Out daily, we also rested much, unencumbered by thoughts. Was it Colorado? Our hosts? Probably both. With much to explore, map in hand, they schooled me on this state. One last dinner and we left for Owl Creek Pass. The screen ahead of us became even wider. The road we looked for north of Ouray became confusing as the miles went on until assured from a welcomed road sign. Much primitive camping on the way, most filled with campers and their ATV's buzzing around. A few miles further down the road, we settled for some dispersed camping right on beautiful Beaver Lake. Sometimes, the search abruptly stopped. I could never explain why, it just felt good and right for us, all base camps to remember if ever back in the same area. Quiet, undisturbed, beautiful scenic views and water being a plus, we set up, and by evening were able to hike around the lake. Spirit in his greatest mood, not that it ever changed, myself missing our conversations with our friends, while at the same time happy and looking forward to spending a few days in such a remote area.

Some mushrooms foreign to me grew in the shaded areas of the path around the lake. They looked as they had been munched on and careful not allowing Spirit to do the same I put him on his leash. The rocks, grayish in the afternoon, turned to gold and their shadows standing tall. The blooming flowers all around us wearing their evening robes, again a postcard setting. Up late in the mornings, settling in maybe a bit too comfortably. That is the object while being on the road, letting it all go by at our own pace and no one else's. We ended up not staying too long. Just a few days. My curiosity never leaving the sight of the map and getting antsy to explore further. We rode back to Ouray for more luxury and say our good byes to great friends before heading further north.

I fell in love with Colorado. A perfect setting for summer times offering much dispersed camping at higher elevation, plenty of shade from many tall green trees, creeks all around us, kind people sharing the same passion for the outdoors. Where have we been all these years? We took Highway 550 north to Montrose. I must have needed something as REI witnessed us spending an hour or so shopping, including some provisions from a food store. Then on Highway 50 towards Gunnison, all along the Blue Mesa Reservoir. How beautiful all this water drawn so blue nearby us with a few campgrounds on its shores which I found out would fill up on the weekends. Crested Butte on my mind we rode past Gunnison through the National Forest of the same name. Contrary to a mindless logic, I heard myself say "We will be spending all our summers in Colorado!" Crested Butte took my heart away, but late in the day we needed to move on and find a space to settle. I knew we would be back many times. The road continued, turning into a mild and well taken care unpaved surface, Highway 12 they called it, not being a highway at all. We found another dirt road which took us to a gem of a space called

Lost Lake. Indeed, it felt as being lost. Calm waters, mountains sprouting from the green layers of pine trees, rugged rocks indecisive in their own directions, all topped with the most intriguing cloud formations at a cool 9,000 feet. I felt stronger than ever. I missed the sunset that night, the sunrise the next morning. There would be many more as long as the sun never stopped its course. All too good to move on, maybe lost, yet, with Crested Butte and Paonia so close, a multitude of roads showed on the map as easily doable. That map those days became a valuable tool. What a stage, all overwhelming as the many others experienced, a slice of Nature much untouched by human hands, only footprints from the few who discovered such treasures. We took roots on our site. We slept late every morning until the sunshine coming through the green fabric of the tent would make me get up. Spirit as usual, knew better. He would not say a word until my first cup of coffee. Kind Spirit.

Only 20 miles away, we often explored Crested Butte. A friendly town, especially towards dogs as most store fronts placed a water bowl by their entrance door. Nice touch. Booming during the summer months in deep contrast with their winter freeze, when only the locals remained getting around with their snowmobiles idle now, versus their cars or the many bicycles present. I found some great Mexican food, good coffee and an open farmers market. We spent all day going up and down the streets, sometimes resting on the many sidewalk benches while watching others. All so harmless and pleasant. I ate well the following days. Fresh peaches for breakfast, nice basmati rice topped with diced home grown tomatoes and ripened avocados for lunch and dinner, plenty of salads. My weakness late into the evening invariably being a spoonful of chocolate peanut butter on a cracker. No avoidance of such a feast. Sometimes with a banana instead. I carried quite an assortment of ingredients which did not need refrigeration.

We hiked a lot those days. Lemon eucalyptus spray took care of the few mosquito friends. Many naps, that daytime hour so pleasant while reading and falling asleep in the coolness of the tent itself under trees. One day, while outside reading, I heard what sounded like a jet passing by, more like a rumble. All of a sudden, the face of the mountain in front of me gave way toppling down in a burst of dust. My camera happened to be right next to me and was able to take some photos, mystified by the event. A first, witnessing such a sight with outstanding notes of thunder as all collapsed and finally rested into a clearing below. So slowly silence came back.

Cesare Pavese wrote: *"Traveling is a brutality. It forces you to trust strangers and to lose sight of all that familiar comfort of home and friends. You are constantly off balance. Nothing is yours except the essential things such as air, sleep, dreams, the sea and the sky. All things tending towards the eternal or what we imagine of it"*. We did own those essentials and ourselves. It seemed enough and plenty. We headed towards Lake City. Highly recommended by my friend KC who used to own a restaurant right downtown. Southbound this time, back through Gunnison, skirting again the Blue Mesa Reservoir where I thought about camping a few days. The weather at the lower elevation being too hot made me change my mind. We picked up Highway 149 following Gunnison River, a beautiful paved road winding through. Such an inviting state.

A squirrel froze in its steps, up he looked, right he went, stopped, changed his mind, one more look, indecision and I lost vision of him. I did not feel a thump nor did I see him in my rear view mirrors. One saved life. Half a mile later, probably one of his long lost cousins, now a bloody mass adorned the pavement ahead of me awaiting the buzzards probably on their way for breakfast. This time indecision took his own life. I looked up and amid the clouds playing, a jet is being followed by his own white trail disturbing the present canvas. Lightning fast it is from here to there, gone so quick. I thought of its 300 or so passengers. Each in their own tight seat with their little fold down tables in front of them, volume of sound knobs tucked into their armrests, more knobs above for light and artificial air. They were probably having breakfast. One of a different kind zapped in the microwaves by attendants in charge. They did not have to wait for the squirrel's indecision to be served. Was the Captain awake? Or maybe dreaming about a limo with a driver wearing a blue cap picking him up from the airport? So many fantasies of the mind took place while riding, often triggered by a certain reality.

We arrived in Lake City, the vibes so excellent unspoiled by any influx of tourists. A quick cup of coffee, and back on the road for the few miles leading to Lake San Cristobal searching for the coordinates given to me for a space to camp. We stopped again when I saw the lake being a definite "wow", also called Santa Maria Reservoir on the map. I found the free dispersed camping very hidden from the road. I had seen across the waters, right on some tall cliffs, a few campers which I knew were enjoying the outlandish views. I decided to check it out before we would set up. Sure enough, we stumbled on a county campground with one site still available a couple feet from a deep plunge into the lake. Must have been at least a few hundred foot drop. At $15 a night, not a bargain, but I could not pass it up even if only for a couple nights as we would just stay still and take in the scenery, and some photos of course. A few days went by, as did cooler nights. I could not make ourselves leave and I renewed our stay. The photos turned out beautiful, but the screen could never share the real moments spent on those cliffs a few feet away from the ledge. Spirit of course, always on his leash. There was no need to take a chance on him getting too close and flying into the waters. My chair supported me for many hours. The wind's murmur passing through the pine trees, the constant changing patterns of the surface of the waters, the clouds never resting while playing their game of dropping temperatures when hiding the sun, this is I thought Nirvana. In my mind, it could not have been anything else.

Moving day came, the wallet could not handle any more nights as much as I would have liked to. The dispersed free camping site not too far, it did not have a view, but right in the trees, hidden, quiet and undisturbed. I enjoyed it a lot. Spirit did too being off his leash, we always preferred that situation. We continued those days not doing much, the temperatures for a summer month perfect and having a hard time getting away from the chair with much reading. KC e-mailed me of a great bakery at the north end of town. I wished as the days went on after our first visit there, he would have never told me about it. It became a routine every morning. Even Old Faithful ended up knowing the way, and if we went closer to noon, besides the bear claws, cinnamon rolls, sticky buns, all still warm out of the oven, gooey, sweet, tasty and light as they should be, I could buy some pizza slices for the evening meal. My chair had to see less of me or I would have to soon buy new pants. As if not enough, on my own without any recommendations while downtown, I stumbled upon an old fashioned soda fountain. Root beer floats so delicious took me back a few years.

We met Dave in town while entering his gallery he shared with a map maker. A glass blower artist and a good friend of KC. KC lived in town for six years and with his outgoing personality and owning a restaurant, everyone most likely had been his friend remembering him. I watched Dave quite a few times while wearing some very dark glasses loaned to me, creating his beautiful pieces of all shapes and colors. It looked so easy and compared it to the delicate pastries I used to create. I knew however it would take years to master such talent, the motions of his artistry so demanding. The spinning with proper heat, blowing, the spraying of colors and sometimes silver or gold on its surfaces. Glass dots, thin threads joining each other so delicately. He could have charged just for watching!

My inability to stay in one place too long surfaced. Bittersweet, torn, words I pronounced sometimes loudly to myself when leaving such a space. I knew too well we had not even scratched the surface of this vast area as many others before. Coming to terms with that notion, I could not fight it, thinking maybe one day it would change. I gave myself the excuse we were just scouting areas for the next times we would come back. Just another version with a bit of truth in it, even though I was making that up.

Lao Tzu once said *"A good traveler has no fixed plans, and is not intent on arriving"*. I knew by then we would never arrive, as when we did, we also left. Summer one more time had its days counted short. South or north? North would be a gamble if the weather turned bad as September just started but not ready to go back to The Oasis. Not yet. We headed north. We could go and get lost around Lander in the Red Desert and again see our friends KC and Mia. Only 500 miles away. Well worth the detour. What detour?

Back one more time to the Blue Mesa Reservoir on Highway 149, then west on a new road for us, Highway 50. It took us through Cimarron, which I always wanted to call "Cinnamon", Montrose, Olathe and Delta. We skirted Grand Junction, unfortunately rode Freeway 70 which took us by Parachute, where I thought about stopping to find out the origin of the name, but did not. We exited the freeway on Highway 13 when we reached Rifle, this time I guessed everyone must own a rifle, silly me. Highway 13 turned into Highway 789 when we crossed the border into Wyoming, with Medicine Bow National Forest on our right. More freeway, 80 by then, and home free when we reached Rawlins heading north on Highway 287. KC always told me September would be the best month for their state.

That area of Wyoming felt like being home. Comfortable, most roads familiar as we looked for the unfamiliar ones which would join them and form a giant web. Cool weather, more perfection on this path of ours. Through the many phone calls with my Mother, I realized how much she wanted to see me. A mutual feeling, but this time she did not want to fly. Being 83, I could not blame her. We arranged for my flight to Munich being at the right place at the right time as KC and Mia offered to take care of Spirit. KC would give me a ride to Denver for my departure and pick me up when I arrived. The momentum changed. As much as I did not like flying and leaving Spirit behind, there was no choice but to go and only few days remained within these welcoming spaces. Much history present not far from Lander and many geological changes had taken place. We stopped in South Pass. At 7,400 feet, about 35 miles south southwest of Lander, nested between the Wind River Range to the north and the Oregon Buttes and the Great Divide Basin to the south, being the lowest point on the Continental Divide between the Central and Southern Rocky Mountains. In times past a natural crossing point, a preferred route for the immigrants on the Oregon, California and Mormon trails in the 19th century. I stood fascinated seeing wagon ruts clearly visible at numerous sites. Chatting with the locals took time while roaming around this little gold mining town. They told me *"South Pass is a cross road in space and time"*. It is that intersection of the past and the present which creates from its ancient days a blur of the facts maybe painting it all a bit as fiction. Present to learn, did it really matter if such fiction would be believed? So much time passed, so much water had run under the bridges of time. The artifacts remained but the residents long gone, replaced now by those of us paying homage to what once was. I read that the first dwellings went up in 1859, serving as a stage, a freight station and a short lived stop for the Pony Express from 1860 to 1861. In 1863, a small military detachment from Fort Bridgers, the 11th Ohio Volunteer Cavalry, manned the station. The outpost ravaged twice by fire in Native Indian raids ended up being locally known as Burnt Ranch.

We had found a needle in a haystack, and a good thing we did as the rain started falling heavily and took refuge in the Mercantile General store while the chatting continued. In 1968 the town celebrated its centennial anniversary, a group of locals banded together and purchased the historic structures. Through donations, entrance fees and events, they achieved their goal preserving one of the best examples of a frontier mining camp, all built almost exactly as a century ago and rightly so, very proud of it. After a great night in Lander, we returned the next day for maybe what many would consider a desolate and eerie ride. A deserted road from Atlantic City to Sweetwater called the Hudson-Atlantic City Road. I felt the loneliness on that road. Maybe the name of our surroundings? Red Desert. Maybe not coming across a single soul, not even cattle? We stopped a few times, noticing some markers here and there. I took a short 360 degree video and called it "In the middle of nowhere". A continuous horizon in a straight flat line. I heard many would get lost in this desert. Nothing there, the silence beautiful and deeper than up Gravelly Range Road. With a knot in my stomach, my thoughts transported me to the plane a few days ahead. A long flight, the urban setting, noise and pollution, crowds, different culture and their customs, all awaiting but worthwhile. The company and the many hugs from my Mother. The future conversations already present in my thoughts those days. I knew I would again try to persuade her moving to Texas, perhaps in Austin, which would be a nice central location to often visit her.

In itself a mild road, not too difficult to ride, bumpy at times with some changes of slight elevations making me curious what would be on the other side of the hills. It would be the same with a light brown road as a ribbon blending in with the horizon, eventually arriving on Highway 287 where we stopped. The few drivers passing by stared at us, probably wondering why we put ourselves through such an ordeal when a nice highway present. I never expected non-riders to understand. We headed towards the modern ghost town of Jeffrey City. When first heard of it, I thought of a modern ghost town as being an oxymoron and it awakened my curiosity. September would be, from all the past years statistics, the last month of summer before the heavy snow started. Dazed, having never seen a modern ghost town, it turned out to be as eerie as our ride. The town began in 1931 with the name Home on the Range. It took until 1957 to become a rich uranium mine with thousands of people streaming in looking for high paying mining jobs. That is when its name changed to Jeffrey City. Modern housing and a state of the art high school with an Olympic size pool. As with many mining towns, it eventually went out of business. We stood there parked in the middle of a main intersection with the grass growing tall through the cracks of the road. The population, which must have been indoors that day, dwindled to 50. The weeds built a natural netting on the tennis courts, all fenced but the gate open, there were no players these days, it did not make any difference. Padlocks on most of the buildings, the usual graffiti, the street signs still up with their paint fading away, no more fire trucks at the station. The church and the bar still open, both always being the balance needed for any town, even a ghost town. I found a flier posted near the main road. A community picnic coming up that Saturday inviting the residents of Split Rock, 14 miles away. I wished we could have attended. No doubt many stories would be heard first hand. We walked some more, right in the middle of the streets, expecting from force of habit to jump aside from an upcoming car. None came.

We rode back on Highway 28, this time a paved road. Taking the Shoshone National Forest road back to Lander, we experienced a totally different scenery. I always say "the other side of the coin", as how could there be desert on one side of the road and luscious mountains across from it? We passed a few reservoirs, Whitten Reservoir, Fiddlers and Louis Lake, much dispersed camping available off Louis Lake Road, and arrived at the Sink Canyon State Park through some switchbacks which reminded me of Bear's Tooth Pass. We went through all of it in a bit of a rush, mostly trying to scout some of those areas for future stays. I was leaving for Denver toward Germany the next day, while trying to ease into the new curves ahead without making a big deal out of it, besides tearing up while thinking about leaving Spirit behind without a choice in the matter.

Plans changed. I would ride Old Faithful alone to Denver storing her with friends. On the road with a suitcase in the chair instead of Spirit, odd, but a better solution than having KC drive twice the round trip to Denver. I experienced the strangest ride ever, and while knowing Spirit not present, I still glanced every so often into the chair. Airport time. Being so out of place, or context if I may use that analogy, in the hub of life for life! Ongoing, moving fast like lines of busy ants, a pace never experienced these past years. I used to enjoy watching people at airports in my younger days. The incessant parade had not lost its pupillary response, not a bit. I did feel having missed a few years of some evolution I could not put my finger on. The one so many were talking about on the Internet which I glanced at sometimes. Clothing never seen before, shoes, pants, shirts and dresses. Even hair cuts seemed a bit unusual to say the least. They would have most likely perceived the same about me if seen at The Oasis, where clothing would be anything clean that day, or sometimes not. No eye contacts, only looks, stares and no smiles. No hand waving, just a constant rush from one gate to another while being pounded by a speaker telling me to never ever let anyone else touch my luggage. Okay, I thought. I passed the security check point having to just about strip off all my clothing and show my laptop, electronics, even turn on my camera to prove it was real and not some weapon of mass destruction. I felt so sad on how all turned out to protect ourselves from each other.

A long flight, too many hours, and thankful for the mindless movies I watched on the little screen in front of me. Tight seats with barely one inch of room to move and the food interested me in its little compartments steaming hot, right out of the microwaves. Of course, I remembered the squirrels. This time I became the traveler above the clouds. The same ones I always stared at from below. Intruding into Mother Nature's dressing room, the changes of costumes took place while moving on at warp speeds. Cotton balls, streamers, plain old fog, cirrus, cirrocumulus, altostratus, altocumulus, cumulonimbus. I knew all those characters now present floating so close.

Being very thankful for the telephone calls allowing my Mother and myself to communicate so freely, the relationship evolved much since the time spent together on the Georgia Coast close to two years ago. We did not have to think alike anymore, much beauty entered our lives while talking for many hours, sometimes every other day, especially on Sundays, a special day for both of us. I knew deep down her moving to the United States might not be in her thoughts. Having been physically separated for so many years I bowed toward it all and accepted her stage as she eventually accepted mine when we embarked into the unknown. Even if I did not agree or quite understood, my acceptance needed to be visible.

Ah! The hugs, the kisses, here, here, one more she would say as we would take a step or two backwards to stare at each other. How sweet a time. Not changed much she did look as though getting tired could come upon her quickly. I hoped I would be in such good shape at her age. The customs freed me and we took a taxi to her apartment. So excited, she could barely contain herself while already planning our outings and where to eat for the coming days. For the two weeks! Quaint and not so little, a two bedroom apartment, one bath, small kitchen but a large living room and dining area. A shrine for Lance. It felt good. I could not easily lift my eyes from his photos and mementos scattered all around.

Present, as in the past, a certain crescendo would take place within our visits. It generally happened the third or fourth day. Nothing being wrong, it just was. My Mother lived alone for a very long time and gotten used to it. In addition, she could only go out for a few hours a day. Maybe three or four at the most, then would want to come back home. I did not have to, as she always told me to stay out, enjoy the town, but her company was the purpose of my visit. I knew there were aspects of life which bothered her. One being patience which now lacked, another being the passing away of Lance and the intense pain created in my life. It took a long time for her to open up on that subject, and at first, I could not understand why she would not want to talk freely about him. She did not want to pain me. Not talking about Lance pained me even more I explained. I wanted to hear about the times they spent together. Details, funny stories, all the stories, even if some brought on sadness and so much missing of my young man only present now in photos. I told her I had become stronger with the acceptance needed, dealing with life as it presented itself. I assured her I could handle it. Once she started, I could not stop her.

We went out for short times just about every day. I saw many dogs. Unlike Spirit, very well trained for the urban environment, as they are allowed to take public transportation and go into restaurants. I did not feel I should or could pet them. Get my "dog time" while so far away from Spirit and lost without him. Munich has a lot of charm, much history within the walls surrounding Marienplatz where cars are not allowed, but the feel for big cities vanished. We ate lunch out every day, she would not let me cook too often. Dinner, which I remembered, was always a tradition in our family as being light. Listening to her stories became the best times, the long ones which besides Lance's went back for over a century involving my grandparents. Proud of her as divorced at an early age, she came a long way and did well for herself while also, as I need to mention, helping us out at times.

Lance always wanted to visit Munich, the open invitation from his grandmother ever standing. He never made it. We walked by an inviting Church one day, and inside stood a myriad of lighted candles in their red holders. I considered them for the departed ones. I might have had the wrong idea about them, but those were my own thoughts. I lit one for Lance and it shone brightly as he did. I sat there watching it burn until my teary blurred eyes overwhelmed me as I turned around and walked away. I felt strong carrying the burden never quite agreeing toward life's path, a reality without a choice. I asked her a very important question. Important to me. "Has Lance's departure changed any values in your life? Has it taught you any new aspects of this stage we all live on? Has it brought on new priorities?" Interestingly enough, painfully for me, her reply was simply "no". She lived into a different chapter, her own distinct time zone. Most importantly, from another generation so rooted in past hardships which to her contained the true meaning of life. I respected that.

One more taxi ride on a very early somber morning back to the airport. I thought of it as a good aspect non-travelers could not pass the security point. It made the long good byes shorter and less painful. One more turning around, watching the small silhouette of my Mother's waving arm as the tunnel towards the plane appeared. Another long flight, one more lonely ride to Lander where I pulled in late and exhausted. This time around, sick and filled with medication trying to combat a flu which materialized a few days before while in Munich. The roads wobbled and so did the ground with every step taken but those brown eyes stared at me that night exchanging an energy unlike any other. All together, three weeks passed, and again, Spirit ran like a madman upon seeing me, stopping a few seconds for a hug, and on more of chasing his dreams which as mine had become an awaited reality. The next day, we started the southbound route. One more time.

There is a certain intimacy I discovered on the road when our SPOT, that live GPS tracker constantly giving away our position, is turned off. I called those times "living behind closed doors". Maybe a result from too much urbanism, an escaped sense of freedom when too many eyes easily stared at routes on the shared web page. An escape within our escape. Only present, Spirit and I. We headed towards our winter evasion. The Oasis. For the third time? Fourth time? I lost track while I missed feeling healthy and energetic as the flu did not let go of me, saddened at the same time by the virtue of a summer which soon would take a past tense. No doubt, even with much of life's schooling, I did not fit very well into the present times. We took it slow. It allowed me to think a bit more than usual while missing the times with my Mother. The conversations, the meals shared, our outings, her memories of Lance, the hugs and even her cozy and comfortable apartment. The solution to have it all never present, regrets part of human nature. The sorrow not having spent more time with Lance and my Mother. Even the thought of moving back to Europe briefly surfaced. The logistics and costs of doing so with Spirit would be a nightmare. The hope my Mother would come and spend if nothing else a few months of her harsh winter never left me.

Our land welcomed us and twenty-four hours later done nothing but cook a very unattractive dinner, letting me wonder how I did it! A boring one of rice and chicken. Afraid to even move and break the present silence, I just sat there while Spirit ran, jumped and finally started snoring while asleep. So much for silence. A new concept in his sleeping: snoring. He would of course never tell me if I did. Blue skies, temperatures around 90, our solar system intact producing the needed power. As usual from the winter rains, the water plentiful, spare bottles of propane lined up for the colder days, the mice in the shipping container moved their blue pellet poison a destination unknown, nothing seemed to have been disturbed even though forgot to lock up the RV sitting immobile. It always felt so huge when entering it, in deep contrast when a few months later I would feel it shrunken. The vegetation grown a bit, I could barely see the roof of the distant neighbor's dwellings a couple miles away on the eastern side and my one and only mesquite tree looked healthier than ever. My Center of my Universe so beautiful and meaningful. Lance on its west side gave us a big welcome while I sat on one of the pecan trunks nearby. All too comfy and no check out time. The thought of writing a book during the coming months already entered my mind.

It did every year, the calendar I sometimes glanced at, showed Lance's birthday arriving, the pain having never subsided. Maybe being something else. It is my own and I dealt with it regardless on those days when nothing else mattered. I know where my priorities always lay. His life, my life, together we made it through highs and lows. Besides him, only our kind friends, my Mother and Spirit. The ladder so tall in front of me.

The temperatures dropped to a comfortable level facing a timeless present. So much so I felt a bit nervous, at the same time being so calm. Those days became gentle waves. I often thought about the many others miles away on their fast paced lives. I often wished everyone would and could live as we did.

> *"We are impoverished in our longing and devoid of imagination when it comes to our reaching out to others. We need to be introduced to our longings, because they guard our mystery. Ask yourself what mystery is being guarded by your longing. Are you taking the time to find out? The time for this never appears. It is discovered". "The Art of Pilgrimage" [Phil Cousineau]*

I could not write this book at the time. Obviously. Four years into our journey, the journal kept its upper hand. It did not bother me as I went with the flow. Not ready to be written, that is simply what I thought. Our rides continued instead within the never ending nearby roads. One of those roads did end one day when arriving at La Linda bridge, one which crossed into Mexico. Man-made cement barriers, high metal gates, warning signs, all impassable and sad to look at. We walked around looking at the dwellings across the bridge where once many lived. Land never felt so divided as that day. Not a soul present, not a dog roaming. Absolute silence toward a freedom taken away not so long ago. We stopped in Stillwell on our way back, a small RV park part of a big ranch today sold. No one around as I sat on the swinging bench reading some of the information put up on the walls. From one ghost town to the next one, such was the ride that day. The last leg of it took us through the park where we stopped at a sign which said Dog Canyon. Behind it a warning "Dogs are not allowed". Not much of all this made my day the world indeed becoming stranger. Happier times were ahead when we pulled back into The Oasis that night. The same week, the notice of "Terlingua Bash" appeared in the local one page paper. I decided we should go feeling too much like a hermit. There would be an open mike afternoon and though to me, the talents of unknown names, a bit of live music would be good. Our friends Paul and Voni, Ardys and Harmonica Bob joined us, chairs set up in the shade, a few photos, everyone took the mike for a couple songs. When over, I heard of a pirate costume gathering a bit further down the road. We attended that event as well, Spirit and I being sociable, enjoying it.

When in Bisbee a while back, we entered Panterra Gallery meeting Chuck and his wife Maralyce, the owners. Chuck is an accomplished photographer. We saw him again at The Oasis when he stopped by while riding his motorcycle on a short journey of his. Our conversations leading to photography, I could not help showing him my best captures. Somehow impressed, he decided to show them at their Gallery. That week was right around the corner and the prints in my favorite Chromira finish shipped, all mounted on hard boards with no frame. Exciting times. We planned the opening for a Saturday evening with food, wine and music. We knew the road to Bisbee. He put us up in a little apartment they owned. A few friends joined us, none of these times could have been any better. My own show. Friday arrived, the day before "that day", and while opening the boxes containing the prints, as we unwrapped them, my heart literally stopped. No mistake being my photos, but all much darker. Every single one of them. As many of somber storms, a disaster. Yes, I teared and did not know what to say when Chuck stood by me totally bewildered. Tragic times with the show within 24 hours. I called the photo lab and told they had been processed without the human touch, from my computer to their computer/printer. A huge mistake. Chuck understood right away what happened and was kind about it all. Kinder than me that day. He came up with the idea to run to the hardware store and have some glass cut for all ten photos. The clear glass and light reflection from above would brighten them up a bit. I think and still believe, anyone else would have canceled the show. It became a busy day with not just one trip to the hardware store, but a few as normally happens with any project. My friends showed up, other riders also on their way to South America, just a coincidence and we all bunked together. The next day, the show a huge success. Happy ending? Not a single print sold for even the coming months. It did not surprise me. Those were not my photos but cheap imitations. Chuck and Maralyce did purchase one. I knew they felt very sorry for me. The photo lab ended up refunding the complete cost of the prints. One more lesson in the school of life.

To most, riding a motorcycle brings on a source of thoughts from one's deepest path of the mind and soul. A car will not do it, convertible or not. Not for me anyhow. A bicycle? I have never tried it for long distances. My closest experience comparatively is sailing. Sailing when all is in the most perfect harmony between Mother Nature's deep breathing, my own ability and the sailboat itself flying through the waves propelled with such natural powers. We experienced such a sail when we left Bisbee on our return with a friend of ours, Shawn. Two glorious days of riding with the winds on our tail. Never stopped for a photo, only a few breaks and fuel. The frames of the present moments were enough developing themselves while adding a contour and shape to those days. The true reality of the show gone sour ended up not being about photos hanging on a wall up for sale, but about the people surrounding us, a time without any regrets. What would be the use for them? As *Henry James* has written *"Things are always different than what they might be"*.

The Day of the Dead, November 2, 2010, had come. One more time we attended upon our return. As always an emotional gathering with all of Terlingua present. Much food, the sounds of guitars, bonfire, candles lit, much conversations. Many being full timers, I wondered how they managed their hot summers and others like us part-timers moving on with the good weather. A short while after, I fell sick again with a bad sinus and ear infection. It would not have been so bad if living in a city, but with the doctor 60 miles away, the logistics become so different especially while staying put and hoping for a better next day. Of course, it does not get any better on its own. On with the inevitable round trip limping to Alpine. Doctor, pharmacy and back. One of the highlights throughout our winter. The yearly cycle continued on. Good and bad weather, hot and cold, all in between just as life.

It turned out to not be the highlight. Debilitating times awaited. Riding off-road and hernias never get along very well. A not so good situation arose as my right side decided to make its move. It happened a couple times before, needing double hernia surgeries. Where to go? How to take care of this? Where would Spirit go? Friends came to the rescue. We left for Tucson to seek proper care. I found a good doctor and surgery scheduled, Spirit in good hands at my friend's house. The positive side of it all? Spirit found himself with a new girl friend while I went under the knife. Maya, my friends boxer. Minutes before surgery, the doctor came by for a final check. By then, my left hernia had started hurting as well a couple nights before. The situation, a bit comical, I asked her "while in there, could you please check the other side?" "Of course…" she said. The surgery lasted a few hours as all, according to her words, a terrible mess. She could not remove the old mesh on either side and I became "double meshed". I smiled at the thought. The word Superman came to mind. It became my third time having this double surgery. To my surprise, they sent me home right away. The doctor's last words while leaving the hospital "I hope you continue riding, but don't come back to see me if you need another double hernia surgery". More smiles.

Healing took time while forced to rest. I enjoyed my friends company, cooked a bit when able to stand up and even watched television with them. Spirit forced to play, his romance went well, he and Maya as a constant show. Eventually, able to ride, we slowly and carefully returned to The Oasis. That is when and where I realized it might have been a mistake. The urban life now 600 miles behind and staring at me, three gallon water jugs, propane bottles, my bags, opening and closing the heavy door of the shipping container, all too much weight for those times. I had not thought this through very well. Spirit moped and yet had to grow some thumbs to help me. The fragility of life, the harshness of our environment, our lifestyle, all surfaced trying to stay in harmony with each other. That winter, quite a challenge to stay afloat.

The tomorrows never stopped, nor did the severe cold fronts while experiencing an indoor end of winter. The word stagnant came to mind. Many books downloaded, more "one-pan" recipes published on our journal, some slow walks throughout the warmest part of the day always taking in the last rays of the sun when present, glows of such incredible colors painting the clouds of indescribable hues. Spirit never took his eyes off me. Amazing how he understood these quiet times. I was surprised we had made it to The Oasis from Tucson. When deciding we would go to Terlingua only about 30 miles away, I made a U-turn, the sitting position jabbing the mesh in the tender areas not yet healed. So much for riding and being Superman. Only then did I remember the doctor having said to stay off the bike for at least a month. Christmas came and my only jingle was Spirit's bear bell always on his collar. I knew his whereabouts from that music he played when moving around. New Years passed. Regardless of how I felt, I so much appreciated being on this land of ours. Those were Lance's days. My young man who loved "nice things" and good food. The sound of the laughter in the kitchen while we cooked, the jokes, the unwrapped boxes while stepping on the gift wraps, all broke the silence those days.

I started making plans for Spring having to keep my mind occupied as another word surfaced, "stale". "*This is a great moment, when you see, however distant, the goal of your wanderings. The 'thing' that has been living in your imagination suddenly becomes a part of the tangible world"* *Freya Stark* wrote. That goal always nested in my imagination but I never really knew of its outcome. I still don't know and maybe never will. I only know the road and "going, gone…".

The rider skidded sideways off the black paved road and onto the dirt in a tumultuous cloud of dust. As he pulled himself out of his hack, he threw his arms up in the air pointing to the skies in a total indignant manner. He could not take a deep breath, his body shaken with every semi-truck going by, its noises, fumes and smells. Freeways! Now, that is creativity, a great concept, probably the best aspect in traveling to keep everyone in tight sequence when going from point A to point B in this fast and furious world of ours. The positive of all this? Keeping many off the favorites tracks he normally pursued. His gaze went into the horizon, that space where he so much preferred to be as he thought for a few seconds abandoning it all and with his dog, start walking and walking some more over the hill. The fences up, he could not. The fences on his physical path which translated too often into one within his mental aspect. Sitting in my chair one afternoon napping, it was a bad dream. As they say, all things must pass and those days did become a memory by the end of winter. The most quiet one we ever had. I could barely sleep the last night at The Oasis before our departure, running away as in the past. I much enjoyed packing those days. I remembered my planning and doubtful of its unraveling. We would instead go with the flow as we always did. Run some errands in Alpine and spend our first night in Marfa, a sort of Art Deco campground for tents as they also rented antique RVs for the night. They did not allow any vehicles on the premises and quickly that thought vanished not wanting to carry all our gear in, a bad concept. Too late in the day to push on past El Paso, we made it to Van Horn and got a room for the night. Time for a long shower, staring at four walls and very little sleep. We made it through El Paso the next day, took the familiar southern route and arrived in

Columbus mid-afternoon. The Pancho Villa State Park seemed inviting. We moved slow not completely healed. I knew from previous times it would take up a whole year for any resemblance of the pain and its discomfort to totally vanish.

Nearing the little town, I saw a couple choppers flying and smoke coming up from further away. I heard gun shots. As we got a bit closer and pulled over, some dark silhouettes ran around in military gear. More shots, smoke. They must be in the midst of filming a movie I thought as I stood up and watched, thrilled about the show unraveling. None of it lasted too long. The smoke vanished, the choppers flew away, sirens were now in the distance and we entered the park looking for a space for the night. I found it a bit crowded, maybe something to do with the movie. After a good night's sleep, we headed to town for much photography among the historical buildings, a nice cup of coffee at the local Bed and Breakfast and heard the truth about the day before. None of it a movie, but a raid by teams of Federal, State and local enforcement officers. The mayor, the chief of police, ten others, while one still on the loose, were arrested for arms trafficking. Columbus is after all a border town. We witnessed real grenades, gun shots and smoke bombs and heard that the SWAT team excelled at their job. I didn't know what to say. I had not taken any photos.

As the conversation went on, it became clear why the campground was cramped. A pleasant surprise. Columbus Furlong Day. A celebration for Pancho Villa when he rode into town from Mexico over 100 years ago. There will be much going on when 100 horsemen from Mexico will meet 100 horsemen from the nearby towns on our side of the border and ride in together. A promising parade. I could not believe my luck while I rode back to camp to get more camera gear. Such good timing. It started with the parade. Two hundred colorful riders of all ages, beautiful horses and their flags. All lasted a long time. Pancho Villa finally showed up, a look alike with costume and all, and as he saw Spirit in his car, he rode off the parade route, came behind us and asked to have his picture taken with him. I love that photo! The main square opened up, a stage for the many singers that afternoon and street vendors selling candies, clothing, boots, you name it. Children ran around, friendship in the air and us in the middle of it. I then found out about the free food. A huge pot set up on a burner and someone making fajitas for 1,000, stirring it all with an enormous paddle. Behind the cook, inside the community building, long tables lined up covered with containers of food of all kinds prepared by the locals. As containers emptied they were quickly replaced with new ones. A constant changing menu with no end to the feast . Memorable moments being at the right place at the right time.

We continued west the next day on a road by then so familiar to us. Passed Animas, we entered the little town of Portal instead of making a left for Douglas. We rode up and down the mountains facing us and camped by the Chiricahuas National Monument. A nice primitive site by a creek, in a canyon which did not see much sun, and cold mornings waiting for some heat to drop from above. The park itself, "a wonderland of rocks", so unique. The Apaches call this space "The land of standing-up rocks". The monument is one of the many "Sky Islands" of the beautiful Chiricahua Mountains surrounded by expansive desert grasslands. Twelve thousand acres of wild and rugged terrain within the protected rock formations. The road to the scenic look out is only eight miles long with not many pull outs. As usual, we avoided the obligatory tourist parked in the middle of the road on a blind curve, door left open, taking a photo or watching some bird with their binoculars. Pinnacles, columns, spires and column rocks. We could not get too close to them, only admire from a certain distance.

Moving on further west, we set up camp near Patagonia. A little town of barely 1,000, many galleries, a hotel being refurbished and a couple restaurants. A pizza joint called "Velvet Elvis". Bad news arrived about my best friend of all times, Bill, who has had cancer for a while, now being checked into hospice. The ceiling always upon us as an open sky dropped on me. We stood still at camp. Any desire to go anywhere or ride now gone. A couple days later, his wife Kammie called me with the final news. Acceptance, understanding, once again many words became useless. Another chapter of life seeing its end, shut down forever. I had a book with me at the time *"Secrets of the Lost Mode of Prayer"* by *Gregg Braden.* One about the lost Mayan culture when simply speaking considered a prayer, when the word "hope" was justifiably not used, but "be into the now" spoken. *"Beyond an appreciation for the things that are simply pleasing to our eyes, beauty is described by wisdom traditions as an experience that also touches our heart, minds and soul. Through our ability to perceive beauty in even the ugliest moments of life, we may elevate ourselves long enough to give new meaning to our hurt".*

I could not do anything during those days. I only sat and stared, feeling the immensity of it all. The world felt empty, uninhabited. A missing and loving soul departed while trying to comprehend how I managed to survive my son and my best friend. Bill and Kammie harbored me for months after Lance passed away, never allowing me to get into the depths of sadness, Bill being the biggest jokester there ever existed. One day, gently, they kicked me out for my own good. They knew it was time to go on and confront the real world. Which I did as here I am writing about it.

We could not go too far as I agreed to teach my "One-Pan" cooking recipes at Overland Expo coming up shortly. Such an off time, but committed with no escape. We set up in Amado after much food shopping and some prep for the scheduled three classes, each with two planned recipes. The logistics being simple, I chopped, prepped and bagged most everything for convenience so as to not waste time during the classes, even rehearsed once and ate it all. I needed to convey the notion one could very easily travel without refrigeration. Of course, no meat or many dairy products which would quickly spoil in the heat of summer. It is about some common sense using shade available for storage, a good insulated soft cooler, or a hard one if in a four wheel drive or car. The recipes are mainly templates as one could and should use their imagination switching ingredients to their likings or availability. The Expo started on a Thursday, we arrived a couple days earlier mentally preparing for the event with always my buddy in tow. Bill's passing away made times harder. I did not want to smile but needed to, not feeling much like chatting either. It seemed going against the grain of a moment when I wanted to be somewhere else wishing for the world to stop spinning until I caught up with all the present emotions. I knew I would regain my balance in the near future, once behind those boulders and monuments reached by the brown dirt roads. Only there could all my senses could pause and emerge above the stormy winds and accept sailing through the grim reality. Those days turned into quite a roller coaster as the presentation started and the crowds showed up.

We knew many of the ones present. The comfort zone ended up being more peaceful than originally thought, and with no further delay showtime took place three days in a row. An awning had been set up on a nice grassy area. The coverage too small as the classes overbooked and felt badly for the ones having to sit in the sun for the duration. It all went well. I fell into the moment very quickly with no thoughts of past or future. Cooking, talking, explaining, all with 60 pairs of eyes attentive on me and Spirit laying smartly in the shade. I called it, and still do, "sharing", without a desire to be catapulted to any level of stardom, but for everyone present to eat better the next time they would be out and around some wilderness. We made new friends, chatted with old ones, watched a couple movies, more classes and more feeding the crowd. It seemed the vendors multiplied from a year ago. Everything to do with the outdoors and this time around, more motorcycles. A bit tight, overcrowded for us and rare quiet times.

I received an e-mail from Kammie while on our way out. *"We said our goodbyes, pledged that we would find each other in another life if it were possible and pledged a love that would never die between us. Once the morphine drip started that day, he was pretty much out of it. His nephew, Cornell, found some BMW races on his iPad and put his headphones on so Bill could hear them. I was holding his hand and I felt it tighten around my fingers and he twisted his wrist like he was giving it the throttle. What a very precious moment that said it all. I only hope that wherever his spirit is, the wind is blowing through his hair as he rides as fast as he can."* Words escaped that day as I myself twisted the throttle.

Sometimes, the ingredients of life seem to be borrowed from a recipe only too familiar, yet never dished out in the fashion we might imagine. We rolled out on Monday morning exhausted from the past days, my own gears emerging overheated. A success for us and for all, but Bill never left my thoughts. He now kept us company with Lance from somewhere up there, certain he would also follow us, his hair blowing through the air as a silent banner throughout the present moments.

And now, where would we go? The path ahead wide open. Sometimes Old Faithful took the decisions as we headed towards Nevada. A little ghost town called Gold Point perched a bit above 5,000 feet, located not too far from Death Valley, that vast desert where we could go back to and explore what we missed. Gold Point, named Hornsilver at one time when it experienced growth and decline is a gem. Population: seven. A livable ghost town thanks to Herb Robbins. We ended up living there for a while on a solitary lot once buzzing with much excitement having been a mining town. I felt being part of the ongoing history that preceded us. All not totally solitary as I could smell food cooking on the weekends, all due to Herb's doings. Gold fever caught up with him when only 15 and lived in Carmichael, California. While panning for gold one day, a few flakes brightened his moments and ignited the passion of his newly found interest which never came to rest. A permanent fascination as I quote him *"I wanted to go where these people lived and see how they existed and what was left behind".* While in Gold Point in 1978, he stumbled on some property for sale. Right then and there, his future became decided. With a friend he met in 1981, they took residence and started rebuilding the town. A few RV sites with power and sewer, restored some cabins, built an outhouse, a shower and the biggest accomplishment, the Saloon on Main Street which used to be the old telephone office. A 16 × 24 foot dwelling, now 16 × 110 foot, also a Museum. It housed artifacts Herb and his friend Walt found and accumulated while on their discoveries of the West. A rare array which took a while to absorb in that immense space. The bar laid out by the front wall, the old manual cash register present, a shuffleboard, an early 1900's pool table and an out of tune piano. Photos of cowboys and old maps covered the walls, old bottles on dusty shelves and an eye popping collection of bric-a-brac everywhere. Herb's food tasted the best on weekends when he cooked for the few that would stop by while escaping the city. After being beat up by the sun all day, bounced around the surrounding dirt roads, I always managed to eat twice as much as I normally would. It felt so right being there, I did not want to leave. We did not have to. Life suited us just fine. Ten hours of sleep every night, a daily shower, a nice make shift outdoor kitchen during the week. Why move? Those were days I took care of Spirit in the mornings before my coffee, being always so late getting up.

They say it is easier for one to find themselves while away from it all. It is. The distractions filled with willingness, the flow of an inner path blending with the physical path, all navigated in unison. Those deserted settings allowed for a display of expressions with no holding back. I was the mirror of myself. I could laugh out loud, cry rivers of tears, speak out with no rebuttals or arguments and renew my faith of life. Present moments with no time frame, deadlines, days or dates. Even the year did not matter and got lost buried underneath it all. Harmony being the main character.

A couple guests arrived one evening during the week and Herb, as an exception, cooked dinner. A brainless decision of mine to attend. Great food finished with soft homemade brownies and ice cream. I had both flavors, vanilla and chocolate. No sense holding back. The conversations invariably hovered around topics such as mines, claims, ore, gold, silver and adventures into deep underground shafts. Everything I knew nothing about. I intensively listened and learned much, a real treat overall. If one travels slowly they will often come upon such treasures. We explored the many surrounding well maintained roads when warmer but never returned to Death Valley. I decided to once again visit Valley of Fire.

Valley of Fire, only a few miles away while riding Highway 95 south and on Highway 15 east, finally Highway 169 south, once again avoiding Las Vegas at all costs. I thought at the time I would find more peace among those multicolored rocks but the space stayed busy being the height of the tourist season. Camping had gone up to $20 a night. I gained more writing gigs from attending Overland Expo, also a couple dog magazines asked me the same and a few companies sponsored us with tires, oil, riding gear and money. The sponsors made up for the increased fees and the lack of payment from the magazines. That aspect, the beginning of a painful lesson while spending interminable hours with editors going over my writing, coming to an agreement, yet turning around and never printing what agreed upon. I remember 16 back and forth e-mails to finally get paid half of my fee. Much later, told by other writers, this being the norm in the magazine industry. I wondered why no one mentioned that fact to me. They sucked the life out of us and none lasted too long. I started using my favorite quote *"I just want to live"*. There would be more nonsense I discovered from that world which put quite a distance between us. A year needed to go by before coming to many more realizations re-enforcing my own quote. I had found my way into an industry where we did not belong.

We did not ache from the influx of tourists, just ignored the constant parade of rental cars, RVs and those long white buses. Slices of urbanism made their way into this unrealistic setting, this phantasmagorical stage. I could not let anything distract me from the surrounding which as in the past took over my senses. *Sir Richard Burton* wrote *"One of the gladdest moments of human life, methinks, is the departure upon a distant journey into unknown lands. Shaking off with one mighty effort the fetters of habit, the leaden weight of routine, the cloak of many cares and the slavery of home, man feels once more happy"*.

We headed north with much time left before winter. Though in years past I had been to Stanley and the Sawtooth Mountains, Spirit had not. I received some really good tips from my friend KC as to where to camp and stay cool all at the same time. We turned our back to Valley of Fire pretty quickly, and 700 miles later arrived by the Salmon River. My directions given pretty clear, off Highway 21 I found 455 and within minutes, realizing most spaces taken, we settled on a nice free campsite. We did not have a neighbor for at least half a mile. Nice trees for shade, a fire ring, ten miles or so from Stanley. A perfect summertime base camp. Setting up never took too long and we backtracked to town stopping at the visitors center. They are generally run by locals and the best source of information. Being a huge area to explore, I wanted to know it all including fishing for the first time in years as able to afford the "Out of State Resident" license. Not moving anytime soon, I knew it would be a worthwhile expense and provide many tantalizing lunches and dinners. Only 60 people lived full time in Stanley and as time went on, we met them all. Smaller than Terlingua, the sign I read said 63, but three moved away as the area recorded the coldest weather in Idaho for winter times, the temperature sometimes dropping to −40 degrees. I could not imagine life throughout that season. There were never tourists showing up those months, and if it happened, the town would not allow them to camp, being too dangerous. Loaded with maps, much information, my license, fishing pole and lures, we returned to camp where we both felt so good knowing we yet had much time ahead of us. My helpful friend always right.

We slept so well those nights. The temperatures perfect, only needing a hat and a jacket when brewing my first cup of coffee on the stove which sounded like a jet plane cutting through the prevailing silence. A day or two later I found the important needs for our stay. Grocery store, showers, laundromat and the library for wifi. The eternal Internet I could not get away from. Cell phone reception being poor, I could barely receive and send out e-mails which would trickle in and out throughout the night from my very smart phone. Fishing days arrived and I found myself excited about catching fresh food. It had been years, but I remembered how to cast and what to look for. The river moved fast and so did the lure which always ended up resting near the banks. It turned out to be not that simple as also trying to find shade for Spirit. Shade, slower moving waters, fish. I needed more tips as to where to go since not catching any the first few days. We stopped at the extremely serious fishing outfitter. If I remember right, the owner told me he lived in the area for over 30 years. Besides pointing me toward the right direction on the map, he showed me the best lures to use. Which I bought. Fishing became expensive, from the start trying to figure out its price per pound, if I would catch anything. I concluded it was the pleasure of fishing, not the catching. That would eventually be a plus.

Track of time was gently being lost as if the tree fell in the forest and no one there, would it make a sound? Was time really time or were we just there? I did look up the date realizing it would soon be the Fourth of July and the little town of Stanley planned a parade. I like small town parades. They always try their hardest. In the meantime, showers, visits to the hot springs, laundry and more fishing kept me busy, Spirit always ready for the rides. I discovered the dredged ponds and came back one evening with six trout. I caught many more, but being too small I gently released them. Of decent size, dinner always present in my imagination while reeling them in. We would often go back to those good fishing holes with no thoughts at all about moving from the area, followed by a sense of comfort as "this is where we belong right now". The Sawtooth Mountains not being a mistake, thinking how different all appeared since those first years on the road when quantity took over quality and we criss crossed the map to no end. Living on the road now took on a different meaning.

The day of the parade arrived and we met more locals while mingling with a visiting population explosion. We fit right in, Spirit always in the middle surrounded by many with cameras in hand, curious about him. Many local colors and Fourth of July a success. Children running around picking up candy thrown from the floats, riders and their horses, the fire trucks, the elected queen for the day and even the dogs parading happily in the good weather. A change from the past and future snow and ice. A couple blocks off Main Street, vendors set up stands selling hamburgers, BBQ and soft drinks. On a makeshift stage a band took their place above the sounds of the crowds and the dancing started. I watched while chatting with another rider in town that day from Boise, and splurged on a cheeseburger with crisp fries.

The present became an intersection, a cross road, an important bridge toward our future. I reminisced on the knowledge acquired those past years. Much reading from books and friends writing, wise words opening up the windows allowing a kinder soul. Many met and meaningful conversations exchanged. Our path chosen out of past desperation, one embraced with nothing else to lose but myself. Such a gift without ever knowing in past times it would lead to a great wealth and understanding of life, even if at times I still questioned its validity, quickly realizing the nonsense of such thoughts. What a process! It had a beginning, yet I would not see the end. The more I knew, the more my thoughts bordered on the less I knew. It often made sense, sometimes not. It did not matter as long as we could live in the now with Spirit as always the best teacher.

Someone wrote us *"If there is a God on earth, He lives in the Sawtooth Mountains"*. How true. I stepped up the ladder those weeks even if without warning a run of bursitis destroyed my left shoulder. The doctor in Stanley stopped by once a month and my timing perfect. I needed to curtail riding and fishing, he said. Not so good news when that is about all we did. I did not follow his advice too well and with my own logic balanced out our riding and my fishing with how much pain I could handle, as eventually, I knew it would go away. It might just take longer. The weather turned cooler, the warm season never lasted too long up north. I began getting up later, waiting for the sun's rays to hit the tent and warm it up They were three layer mornings attending to my coffee in the vestibule where my kitchen was set up. Spirit did not seem to mind as I could hear his snoring sometimes even over the penetrating sound of the stove. The chirping of the birds always took over when the flames were finally turned off. They and the pine trees kept me company until I awoke Spirit out of his sleep. I started calling him "the lazy bum".

It seemed ironic always being "just when I was going to...". The bursitis became a hindrance. I mapped out some new trails toward lakes not yet visited, marked a turn off opening to a meadow carpeted with flowers of all different colors and heights, more highlighted destinations on the map. It all waited. Not far from where we end up fishing most of the time, we took a tour of the Yankee Fork Gold dredger. We passed by it a few times and comically so large I did not see it, or more likely thinking "that" could not be the dredger. Built in 1940, it dredged those ponds I fished in, extracting gold while I only caught fish! The size of a three story building, built in five months, it floated on two giant pontoons manned by only three workers. A fourth worker called the "Gold Man" came by every few days being the only one allowed near the gold and the vaporized mercury they used for the precious metal to stick to the chutes. A fine job. He never lived too long. The dredger made its way digging for five and a half miles and back. An amazing set up considering the working conditions, especially in winter when the building without insulation saw temperatures dropping to –50 degrees. All with an incredible noise level and wet environment.

Custer Day arrived. A nearby yearly celebration. I knew the way, but because of the crowds present we left Old Faithful at the dredger and took a shuttle to the little town of Custer. A day filled with activities. Dutch Oven cooking, gun fight reenactments when I walked away with Spirit considering his fear of gunshots, home made ice cream, gold panning stations for mainly the children and much history learned. That is where I heard the possession of raw gold was illegal during the mining years. Because of such a law, they used to just wrap it in plain newspaper for shipping. No one would touch it, stealing never being a worry of the company. Try that today! A great time with the help of the Idaho Wilderness Rangers, all very friendly and helpful ready to tell the ancient stories.

Both at camp and on the road, mornings would shine towards new bright days. They decided the path of the upcoming times with past decisions thrown on the wayside as they really did not by then matter much. Times when the mind started taking inventory of the present figuring out which step I stood on while absorbing Mother Nature's canvas. Nothing due and nothing owed, thinking, naively I must say, this is how society should have been from day one but aware of the contrary as once being part of it myself. While sitting and just being, I would mentally contemplate the many buzzing around in a hurry, putting on the last touches of a breakfast while running late, locking up their four walls with an alarm to shield their possessions from others, cars being unlocked, the wheels starting to roll towards the various destinations often hours away in the midst of traffic, where most would again lock themselves up in a working environment enabling them to repeat the cycle. An institution programmed by society with a resemblance of survival, never understanding none of it was not a rehearsal. Necessity drove many. For others, greed held its carrot dangling, the mail brought on the cause of this human turmoil with numbers never clearly correct to anyone's eyes. Bills. The luxury of 800 channels watched with stupor on a wide screen television itself not yet paid for. The envelope demanding a third mortgage as the chrome Hummer drops off the children at private schools dressed in an impressive fashion adorned with $200 Nikes. We remained absent from that circle, exited, left the building. That aspect of life which would continuously crumble from the traps humanly created only to immediately rebuild it when the fads hit the opening page of everyone's Yahoo too present and updated by the second. The hands tapping impatiently on the steering wheels, the horns sounding as extensions of inner cries, some middle fingers protruding through dark tinted windows. Worse of all, over the latest and loudest "thump... thump... thump..." music, the minds would sink into the darkness of a choleric state losing control of their own emotions, only wishing instead, having the present ability for some punches which in thoughts could solve, wrongly so, the waves of the present moments. I did write "naively".

The backdrops were of the most humanly possible beauty. The spaces of serene textures as one would think the mind could only sink in and find a certain absolution enunciating a signature that would remain for times to come. The main paved roads unfortunately, as the season slowly came to an end and many present for those last days, often annoyed me due to the tailgaters too close for comfort. I could see them in my rear view mirrors. Their eyes so clearly like pin balls going back and forth from their speedometers to us, and sometimes even glowed like little balls of fire. I could only imagine their thoughts and words. When we would arrive at a straightaway, double yellow line or not, changing gear with a cloud of smoke they passed us. Then of course, stopped a few miles ahead, vehicle mostly on the road, window down and door ajar on the traffic lane taking a photo. Soon after, the game started over. I seriously started accepting the gray areas surrounding us. I heard a great quote which I would often hum *"One needs to choose their battles"*. A battle I wanted to participate in never existed. Not even with the diesel truck driver parked next to us with his engine left running while the smoke of his exhaust directed at Spirit. How could I see the humor in all of this?

Seasons changing. Nothing would stop that, just as nothing would slow us down while heading south to The Oasis, nowhere else attracting me with such a pull. Our own space. Private, undisturbed, no bumpers present. None tangled up. There would be much to do this time around. Piled up mail, much paper even if the few bills were paid electronically, the shipping container, Big Green Giant, a big mess in the RV. I wished it would be a camper with no engine instead since I would not drive it. Hindsight! This was also time to reconstruct our journal. So many asked me for the "One-Pan" recipes. My friend and webmaster Justin set up a real nice on-line store, each priced at 99 cents a download. Very few ever bought them. Cost of living kept going up. It would have been a nice influx of income for our fuel. I set them free for one week. Hundreds went out the door. I had no comments, only thoughts. I guess free is good, one should not get paid for their labor anymore. Not quite learning my lesson, I opened up an on-line T-shirt and merchandise store with of course Spirit as the hero. That notion did not fly very well either. The same for my photos through my Internet on-line gallery. So much push from readers, yet, very few bought. Contents did not matter, marketing being the key and I was not ready or willing to dedicate my nights and days in front of a computer screen hammering into people's heads to please, pretty please, buy my photos, recipes or merchandise. It all kept me busy for a while.

While Skyping with my Mother, the conversations went on sometimes for a couple hours. Once a month, I brought up the subject of her moving here, visiting for winter times. Here meaning maybe Austin. Spirit and I even went there for a few days during the holidays to check it out while attending a Christmas open house at the local BMW motorcycle dealer. I called rental and leasing agencies. Searched for neighborhoods where she would not need a car. She started leaning positively towards the idea. As long as she could escape the harsh winters of Munich I would be happy, trusting she would be as well. I kept having visions of her slipping on the ice and breaking a hip. I never knew how she could handle those winters at her age all by herself. Tough woman. All turned out so busy it became a must to at times escape from The Oasis. Terlingua Abaja became my favorite space to camp in the park and we spent quite a few days and times enjoying those nothing moments as I called them.

"The soul would have no rainbow if the eyes had no tears". ~ Native American quote ~ The words appeared throughout my reading on Lance's birthday. The past years on the road taught me to live without him. The emotions never left and never will. I remained aware of that fact, yet, a new calmness appeared on my path of acceptance. I could no longer imagine us anywhere else on that day. Ever present the question mark if the decision taken to leave it all behind years ago had been the right one. The same query as on day one. Human nature dictated such questioning. Spirit and I alone in the center of this desert on Lance's birthday. A picture in itself. One I started to cherish while being undisturbed on a day which brought such tranquility. Lance had been an old soul in his young body with so much pain during his last years, but never letting it overflow into his surroundings. I could not have been as strong as him. Me, the father, he the teacher. He is the one who gave it all and erased himself for me to regain the true character of the life we lived within.

Familiar winter as the cycle started over. Riding back towards the destinations experienced the years before with only few changes present. New stores, old businesses gone, some new faces which like us stumbled on Terlingua and magnetized by it could not yet leave. Generally musicians who ended up playing in local establishments to make ends meet. We rode River Road a few times, other familiar ones as well. I always wanted to leave but the mental choices brought me back here. West would be Arizona or California. East meant the Panhandle, Louisiana and back to Florida as the Georgia mountains would often be snowed in. Spirit would gain total freedom here and so did I. His months to enjoy clowning around and showing off his agility. "My crazy dog". One of the names I used for him. I cooked a lot as we picked up a new sponsor who sent us a solar oven which turned out to be a marvel on sunny days. Even the food tasted better as it had no hot spots and cooked everything so evenly. My Dutch Oven also of some use though slowly running out of wood. If bought locally they wanted a fortune for a single cord. I found out about a pecan orchard 100 miles from The Oasis, where one could cut their own for a penny a pound. I did not have a chain saw and could not find a loaner. Whenever I met someone who owned one, they asked the same question, "Have you ever used a chain saw?" When I said no, they always replied "My homeowner insurance will not cover you". I gave up on that solution thinking I might some day out of need switch to briquettes.

Most evenings, the skies caught on fire and I would sit with Spirit and take it all in with an image floating at times in my head. An old man with long gray hair to his waist, wrapped with a white sheet holding a long wooden cane menacing the skies in an upward motion. His dog sitting and howling next to him. I wondered if that would be us some day. The arms of the sunset's glow reaching in depth grounding me, the messages so distinct. The mountains surrounding us with their tentacles of rocks cutting through the horizon, the silence I would sometimes forget to listen to from a mind too busy while being reminded of it, the first star in the evening's breath taking birth. How could we ever leave such a stage?

We took little journeys here and there. A few days in Del Rio on Lake Amisdat, or Reservoir, depending on which map I looked at. A week up the Texas Hills while visiting a motorcycle museum, the hills being a different stage. The leaves changing colors added another perspective towards fall and winter. Sabinal, Utopia, Rocksprings, Kerville, Mountain

Home, Camp Wood, Barksdale, we saw them all. And we came back to our solitude, happier than ever.

> *"You are what you are seeking. You are standing at exactly the place towards which you have been traveling—for seven years or seventy years or seven hundred years. Your reality is within you, it is not somewhere else. But to understand the point, sometimes it takes years. You knock on many doors before you come to your own door and then, you are puzzled because this is the house you had left and this is the house you have been searching for. It takes to realize that which you are. Basically there is no need: you can realize just now, this very moment. But to realize it you will need a certain maturity, a certain centering, a certain awareness, a certain silence." [Osho]*

I never stopped writing our journal, neither reading many books. January 2012 rapidly came along after a quiet Christmas and New Year's Day, the scenery at The Oasis always generous to be with. Quieter even more on the 26th reliving Lance's last day, feeling it all so strongly as time passed did not matter much. Life challenged me to relapse into oblivion. I did not. The acceptance became stronger with each hour that went by, the memories so strong and real. Spending a long time talking with my Mother that day, she realized again the good aspect for both of us to confront those times instead of keeping them all bottled up. What *Jodi LaPalm* wrote resonated in me: *"Nothing can describe the overwhelming grief that takes over like a virus, deadens each cell of the body, and consumes every second you breathe. You owe no apologies to anyone, especially yourself, for taking the time to find a way out of this"*. The thirst for the road became my way out and time approached to pack up and go. The comfort of The Oasis would be left behind, a new comfort would take its place. A different mental one. We both knew the drill and what to do by then. We would have a loose plan A, yet plan B and C in my mind always on the alert. A ritual while on the road. By mid-afternoon we began seeking a space to rest for the night, leaving me time to cook dinner, take a shower at an RV park for maybe a couple dollars or at a small laundromat in some small village. Most had showers. We carried enough water and fuel just in case. Extra food. Staying away from the mainstream. The excitement of the last morning never dwindled down. I often wondered if it was normal to feel as such, followed by a quick rebuttal "what is normal?" In ancient civilizations, when a family while traveling was ready to move on to their next destination, when everything got packed, all said and done, they would while geared up and ready, sit for a bit and think. They glanced around to check if they had forgotten anything envisioning the road ahead and their destination only then prepared as already traveling with their soul. Something I started doing even if Spirit did not quite understand why. Maybe he did.

Rolling down the road turned out being much different this time around. We now also had a used Honda Element designed as a pop up camper, all wheel drive and lifted a couple inches. The camper itself only took a minute to set up and I could sleep above by climbing through the sunroof. The rear seats having been taken out, between the trailer on which Old Faithful was secured and the rear of the car, much space became available to carry more "stuff", including a large cooler. In reality, we did not have more as everything went in boxes instead of bags. We remained without refrigeration as I used the cooler for food storage. The convoy, as I started calling it, would be our base camp wherever we went. While being between point A and point B, we now had the freedom to park just about anywhere and have a good night's sleep without having to set up the tent which we still carried. We would use it for a living room and kitchen when we stayed in one place for longer times. A strange feeling to drive versus riding. I did not like it very much as a certain guilt being a bit too comfy took over me. Yet, when future days came along with bad weather such as rain and hail or going through areas where the temperatures neared 100 degrees, happiness took over being sheltered. It only took Spirit less than a minute to start enjoying his new well cushioned bed.

We spent our first night in Marfa, after seeing the "Marfa lights" bouncing around mysteriously as no one ever found out how they came about. It became too easy to set up while in town parked right across from a laundromat with wifi. I started liking the camper that same night. One thing for sure, we moved on much faster and listened to a lot more music. I did not mind. In familiar territory, El Paso passed us by, we took Highway 54 northbound and stopped at the Three Rivers Petroglyphs site in New Mexico. A site ran by BLM with free camping for us. The area had an interesting history with over 20,000 Petroglyphs from 600 years ago identified in the area drawn by inhabitants of a nearby village, all descendants from the Jornada Mogollon prehistoric Indian culture. We fell very quickly into what I call "the homeless groove". With great weather I did not even bother with the tent, only setting up a fold out table to be our kitchen. We hiked the rocks the next day, and the following day. The hosts at the campground turned out to be very friendly and we chatted daily. It was unfortunate to find some Petroglyphs drawn by modern hands, in other words, called graffiti. They tried so hard to keep an eye on the visitors so such would not happen, but quite difficult to do it all day. Fortunately, the path making the loop up the hill did have opening and closing hours. It always baffled me as who in their right mind would desecrate such a space.

A great find a couple miles up the road. A little church called Santa Nino de Atocha. I often asked myself if all this could be a dream of a dream as I ended up spending most of the day in the Church, while Spirit waited outside in the shade. I lit several candles for Lance amongst the many artifacts, photographs of children, baby shoes, toys, flowers. The sun played all day while moving around and peeking through the colored stained glass windows. A man stopped by in the afternoon. He came in and prayed. I went outside with him when he was done and we started chatting about his own life. He and his family lived a few miles away when working as a hired farm hand. The business went under and they all moved to Alamogordo. None of them happy there including his wife and the children. He became very emotional and cried freely in front of me. I tried to console him the best I could telling him a bit about my own life, about Lance. I succeeded in making him appreciate his own family, even though they did not live anymore where they really wanted to. I went back into the church after he left, but not before he thanked me for being there. He understood and promised to hug his family that night as I would not. There was indeed a reason why we spent the day in Church.

We stopped at the White Sands National Monument. What a sight! The dunes seemed to be slowly moving on as we did. Blown by the constant winds, they overflowed over the shoulders of the sinuous curved paved roads. Sand particles, as us, where one would think nothing grows, but some greenery protruded here and there as our own souls when they expanded. Dunes and more dunes. Each granule becoming the seed for the waves formed, scriptures from the incessant winds blowing night and day. We avoided stepping on the drawings so delicately marked while being taken back by the vastness of it all. Constant movement and yet going nowhere. I felt a part of them, slowly moving within the same elements. As with the storms which will descend upon the sand ripples, the rain will erase the fine sketches drawn. The daytime glare was blinding and as night time fell, the clouds played with their palette of colors. I stood there as my heart beat faster. I could barely contain myself on this powerful stage. We wandered around often blown away waiting for calmer minutes. Two hundred seventy-five square miles of desert, the world's largest gypsum sand field. A sign read "Like no place else on earth". An unforgettable experience.

We visited Fort Stanton on a darker day. The word Fort equaled wars. I never felt any glory in wars always reminding me of a somber cloud depicting everything humanity should not be. Without touching political entities, it has been my opinion, maybe a naive approach to how this earth, world or universe should be. Fort Stanton disturbed me. It does have a long history. The early cultures lived along the Bonito River leaving behind rich archeological evidence of human occupation. As time went on, Spanish and Mexican settlers established communities in the nearby area, long before the United States sent the military to protect the settlers from the indigenous Apache Indians who claimed the land as their own. Named for Captain Henry W. Stanton, the Fort was established in 1855 as a military fortification through 1896. Disturbing aspect considering the land indeed belonged to the Apache Indians. The clerk at the visitor center had a smile on his face when chatting about it. I did not. Empty and deserted that day, the winds picked up creating turmoil, the space came through as being very eerie. Fifty-three buildings, all empty, only cobwebs residing in every corner, the power and water off. At one time, the first Federal Tuberculosis hospital during World War II, it interned both German and Japanese prisoners. So many walls to keep everyone in and not out. Kit Carson lived there, so did John "Black Jack" Pershing, Billy the Kid and the Buffalo Soldiers of the Eighth and Ninth Cavalry. Some still resided in the nearby cemetery where we stopped.

Returning to camp became a breath of fresh air. A few days later, after a hug from the hosts, we left for Chaco Culture National Historic Park. We joined Highway 40 west of Albuquerque, then north on Highway 371, east on the deserted Highway 9 and the last 20 miles of the worse washboards on Highway 57 north by Seven Lakes. Washboard always meaning fast or slow. I was driving, trailer and Old Faithful behind, I took it slow having the whole day ahead of us. The adventure started when we arrived. Being a National Park, the only choice to spend the night was a campground. Full, I spoke with the Ranger in charge and he gave me the one and only option, to drive back the 20 miles where there would be a campground on the side of the road. I had seen it and this was not going to happen. Of course his first question had been "Do you have a reservation?" I did not comment on it. We drove through the campground anyhow, noticing the large space occupied by the hosts. Large enough for two buses, there would be enough room for us to park. That is all we needed. My frustration rose as they refused, not wanting to share their space. Having come from the south, I decided to explore the northern route and to make matters worse, a few miles away started a Native Indian Reservation where I did not want to camp, not without permission. I should not be writing this as our camp space has been kept a little secret, but here it is. Barely half a mile exiting the northern entrance is a nice unpaved road on the left going uphill. It looked inviting, but I could not see behind the crest if there would be enough room to turn around once going up. Parked slightly off the main road, Spirit and I took a hike and I discovered it flattened and the shoulders wide enough to make a U-turn. Looking closer at our Benchmark map, this road went along the power poles which appeared once we cleared the top and it returned back into the park. That is where we ended up camping a few nights while our visitors, a few cows, woke us at times. The concept of a million acres with two square inches to camp on became a ridiculous one.

The one person very surprised the next morning when driving back to start exploring the monuments, who else? But the Ranger himself. I knew he wanted to ask where we camped. I could tell from his expression, as early in the day, we could not have taken those 20 miles of washboards round trip. He did not. We lingered for a few days visiting one community after another as the dwellings left me speechless considering the fact they did not have metal tools when all of this was being built. It started in and around the year 800, lasting more than 300 years. The scale of the architecture monumental as the complexity of its community life, the high level of social organization, all with a far-reaching commerce creating a cultural vision unlike any other seen before or since. The present wild beauty of this high-desert landscape had long winters, short growing seasons and marginal rainfall, an unlikely place for a major center of thriving culture. The masonry techniques so unique for their times, the massive multiple story stone buildings contained hundreds of rooms and unlike the practice of adding rooms as needed, all planned from the start, the structures oriented to solar, lunar and cardinal directions. Even lines of sight between the great houses allowed communication. Sophisticated astronomical markers and water control devices surrounded them all.

That time of the year for the "One-Pan" cooking classes at Overland Expo approached. They moved the location and it took place at Mormon Lake, near Flagstaff, Arizona. A much cooler area than Amado as in past years. We arrived early and camped a few miles away until the show would start while we explored the area under perfect weather. We found a nice quiet campground called Pine Grove. They always are during the week. We moved to the Expo site after riding the local roads and relaxing for a few days under the abundant shade of the pine trees. Others began to arrive as we continued taking advantage of the tall trees and secured a perfectly located site. The excitement slowly started to built as other wandering souls appeared. The vendors trickled in with their vehicles of all sizes and colors hauling the many goods which would be up for sale. It turned out we were right in the middle of what they named The Moto Village. Quiet quickly replaced with the noises common to such affairs. My classes grown larger with more chairs needed, the canopy covered a bigger area than the previous year. Once again, I became the teacher with two stoves and a couple pans. They called it a success. Camp became crowded as too many insisted on inviting everyone else to share our space, privacy even for just a few minutes lost as a booth was erected only a few feet from us. Tensions built up. Many so friendly before the show, all of a sudden only wanted to be noticed and attract the crowds, going as far as pulling away from us the ones we talked to. I was only there to share, not to sell unlike everyone else. I quickly lost my balance, Spirit ended up being sick the last two days and changed his diet to plain rice for him to hold his food down. All became too much for him, including kids around us screaming and running, tripping on tent cords, bouncing off our trailer, all while the parents too busy trying to make a few dollars or create a name for themselves. Awakening times, I knew then this was never going to happen again as much as I enjoyed seeing familiar faces and a handful of true good friends. All too much of a compromise.

The weekend ended up being a real eye opener, a most important pivotal time throughout the journey. I am sure for Spirit as well. I realized how commercial the "adventure" enterprises had become and that included motorcyclists. It resembled an "industry", everyone now an overlander. I could not stand the word anymore. All the booths displayed an over saturation of gear. So much of it not needed. It just looked good. Some of good designs, most as they say "to make a buck". The saddest, and is to this day, being the transformation of the crowd surrounding us. The ones I thought of as good friends, realizing how loosely that word was used. We did get lost among the thousands of attendees who came in waves and some left touching our lives, even if for just a few minutes of conversations. What more could I have given them but our honest selves, my one and only face. I never carried a mask and we did not need a megaphone to attract anyone. We did not live an imaginary life, our journal written weekly, sometimes more often, told an honest truth, a constant therapy and my counselor. How ironic I found that the bullhorn on its highest volume seemed reserved for the ones covering fabricated adventures, others who have had their own journey in years past, yet wanting to bank on it and continue wearing an imaginary medal so not needed in life. I knew many of these riders because I sometimes bumped into them on their routes. Most portrayed a made up stage and I could not understand that notion until later on. So much being the acts of a whimsical play which in real life never took place.

A magazine owner, his editors and a few more I provided articles also camped nearby. The ones which flatly refused to pay me sums we initially agreed upon. Just because. I was done with them. Best decision ever taken as another circle finally closed while we stepped out of it to once again regain a freedom without any commercial entities. No more magazines, interviews and as much as I supported them, and still do, no more Overland Expo. They would not see us again. I sent out "Thank You" notes to the ones who refused to pay us. I thanked them for waking me up and letting me see the present reality allowing our escape from their stage. They could not suck the life out of us anymore and the same, ironically, turned out to be true with some "so-called" friends, having been thinking a lot about our friendships. With time, they became aware of my decision. The volume of my e-mails diminished leaving present only our real and true friends allowing me more time to nurture such relationships. Amazing times as my smile became permanent thinking about it. So many vanished, the benefits of rubbing elbows with us disappeared. I never heard from them again. Ever. I felt so much lighter, for lack of a better word.

All things must pass they say and the journey continued. We headed towards The Glacier in Montana where we had never been. My friend KC again offered some tips for us. I dipped in my own valleys at times while on route. It seemed I could think more while driving even if not quite totally sold on the concept of trailering Old Faithful. Some days the past resurfaced, the ones having to write down my true feelings, let them out, uncap the bottle and pour it out. As I still do.

> *"If my tears had colors tonight, they would be red. Empty spaces as myself feels as such. The years have gone by and yet the hurt has not. Am I weak or was I too close to my child and cannot let go. Unable to go through this present sometimes, the bottom has never stopped from slipping away and losing a footage never too well planted. Damn it hurts. I have to let the words out, I cannot otherwise even take a step. Must be the dark times of my day. The ones behind the*

curtain. Tired, my eyes half closed, his form plays an incessant motion as a dance unfocused on my horizon. Nothing really matters, only this dirt under me and the skies above, my buddy Spirit, my Mother and my true friends. I so much wished I had a twin just like me who would truly understand the corruption of the present moments" ~ June 4, 2012 ~

A straight shot north 1,000 miles away. We arrived from the east, and upon entering East Glacier, the sight of the white capped tall and raw mountains lifted me up. One of those exciting times. An area when in August of 2005 eight inches of snow fell. The definition of unpredictable weather and ready to explore the surroundings of those glaciers descended from the ice ages of 10,000 years past. They call it "The best care killing scenery on the continent". It took a while to get the lay of the land. I did not think it would even be possible to cover the complete park and its vicinities in one visit. Driving to the closest lake, we checked out Medicine campground and quickly turned around, the space a zoo with each campsite overtaking the other and I could hear the loud vocal roars from the lakefront. I decided to follow my instincts as being early in the day; I enjoyed trusting them. Sure enough, on Highway 2, right at Marias Pass Summit, I found a little semi-primitive campground away from the road. Only ten sites, most unoccupied, all with some shade, the forest as a background and many trails. Some of our friends, the mosquitoes, showed up every day around sunset time. We used our big tent as a living room while reading a good book or writing for those couple hours when our friends visited. I read *John Muir*, so appropriate: *"Climb the mountains and get their good tidings. Nature's peace will flow into you as sunshine flows into trees. The winds will blow their own freshness into you, and the storms their energy, while cares will drop off like autumn leaves".*

We did endure some storms while Sherpa, the name given to our vehicle, ended up being a welcome addition. I would never think badly of it again. We got spoiled and let it be. I felt we deserved it after all those years in a tent. A tent, however, towards which I have never lost its romance. A thin cloth separating us from the bad stormy weather, the cold nights, cool naps in the shade on hot days, an odd concept when one thinks of a house with thick and wide layered bricks. The storms lingered a few days, heavy rains, hail, violent winds, lightning, thunder. I started wondering if we were at the right place at the right time. In mid-summer I did look for cooler weather, but not over the board as then. One morning it all cleared up. Old Faithful dried off, we geared up and headed through the park to ride Going to the Sun Highway via Logan Pass. That road really did it for me. Achieved in 1932, even with today's standards and technology, an incredible undertaking. Winter left behind some damaged sections, portable traffic lights were few, flaggers and road construction crews working hard. I enjoyed those breaks while getting off the bike, taking photos, checking up on Spirit and waving at the driver ahead who just passed us, no doubt late for an imaginary appointment to nowhere. Such wave generally not returned as I could see the driver slumping in his seat probably realizing an embarrassing moment. Traffic was the price to pay while being within one of the most beautiful parks in the country during the height of its season. Much snow welcomed us on the summits, ten foot banks, some already melting and creating waterfalls gushing at high speeds through every nook and cranny imaginable. Sometimes they shot out from a hole on the side of the mountain in constant motion creating silver bands glistening under the sun.

The rains came back halting our rides, the weather a constant cycle. We both end up sleeping 12 hour nights. It really did not matter much anymore as the notion of being on the road changed from the previous years. Looking at the past highlighted routes on our maps, I realized, with much enjoyment I must say, we had slowed down in our movements criss crossing the country, living on the road taking on a different definition. Of course the blue skies came back and this time, later in the day, we rode again through Logan Pass without a single car in front of us. The workers had gone home and I shot a video of the ride with the camera mounted behind Spirit. I still watch them as I ended up cutting it into three individual parts.

Fueling in East Glacier, I bypassed my own rules about concentrating on my routine. I started instead chatting with a couple motorcyclists new to the area. We took off with a full tank, and about a mile or so down the road, my phone which always stayed under the clear cover of my tank bag was now missing. After checking my messages I obviously forgot to put it back. We turned around and went back, but it was nowhere to be found. I borrowed a Sheriff's phone to call myself, thinking perhaps I would hear the ringing while in the parking lot, or maybe someone found it and would answer. It could have not been too far. No help as it rang and rang until my recorded message came up. Searching some more I found it on the ground, right by one of the vehicle exits. Now a lot thinner and the glass shattered. So much for that phone. We rode to Great Falls the next day, the closest Verizon store. It turned out I did not have insurance and for the sum of half my Social Security check, I bought another one at full price. I could not even renew my contract and get a price break on it. Those were the rules at that time. The clerk set it up for me, my passwords worked, my e-mails trickled in. This is when I will use the expression "Not a happy camper".

We turned around and while headed back to camp I decided to pull over on some grassy area and read my e-mails.

> "Ara. I love your website, pictures and Spirit. I too [as Lance did] have terminal cancer and when I am down, all I do is pull up your website. I am sure Lance was thinking of you as I am of my children and try to encourage them to do all things right and true and keep the Lord in your day. We do not know why these things happen but there is a higher power who has a plan. I am certain you were meant to help

many people as you are doing, I am just saddened that it is this way. I love your pictures. When I became ill we had a 5000 mile trip planned through the west for I have never seen other states and have always loved history; but we could not take it and won't get to go. So, dear Ara, ride safe, free and blessed for many of us pray for you. Many hugs to Spirit." ~ Jane ~

I stopped breathing. I would have fallen if not already sitting. The reel of life played in fast backwards motion, frames juxtaposing, a slap awakening me as at the same time a fog settled in and the clarity of the day went away. I teared up and choked on the words. What were my complaints? A broken phone? Too cold those last days? A few mosquitoes? Storms while having to sit endlessly at times in a tent? I felt ashamed of myself having lost touch and straying away so quickly, softened and only looking for the silver lining, forgetting what truly was of importance. Simultaneously, was I happy? glad? delighted?... that my humble journal, my own therapy helped someone else. Honored, that was the right feeling. I wrote to Jane. She never replied. My thoughts remained with her for a very long time afterward. Other e-mails through the years also came in with parallel thoughts or from parents who themselves have lost their children and called me courageous. I began feeling responsible for the well being of many, and at the same time, I never called myself courageous. To me, plainly a choice of life to either succumb dwindling away or stand up and confront as Spirit and I did. Within the silence of the forests I kept hearing for days the grumbling, the groaning and the bemoaning of society for nothing worth anything. Stop, I wanted to yell. Stop and grow up. Think of what matters. But no one stopped for Jane, for Bill or Lance. I did. The journey resumed with reshuffled priorities. Our destinations, the mental ones, all shifted unwillingly with the grasp of its reality as when reading such words. I wanted "to do" for others and at the same time "I had to do" for myself to keep my head up above my own stormy waters. What do we do? Where do we go?

Those questions would be imprinted in my mind. I knew the answers, sometimes tough, doubtful. I needed to trust myself better than I did and keep my faith of life, as all I had to do was follow the spirit which guided us those past years.

The cycle of the weather turned out to be a game and we always bolted out under prevailing blue skies blending in nicely with the crowds. It really was not that bad after all. People to chat with. Everyone of course curious about Spirit as if he was the star of the park! We ended up in Polebridge after a couple e-mails at the insistence of KC. I will always thank him for this one. Yes, another bakery and I must say, the absolute best, #1 on our journey. Maybe of all times? A tiny town on solar and a couple generators, a few structures, easily reachable on a road which paralleled the park's boundaries called North Fork Road. I was blown away by the quality of their baked goods and did not have enough knowledge of adjectives to describe them. Flakiness, the tastes so memorable, their freshness as they kept showing up on trays right out of the ovens, along with twisters each of a different smell. Huckleberry Bear Claws, Chocolate Chip and Cream Cheese turnovers, Croissant rolls with Feta or Ricotta Cheese, olives, artichoke hearts and so much more that a state of confusion came over me. I stepped back the first time around to regain some form of consciousness. Primitive camping as we liked it and the bakery became a daily stop. It was a space for others who also had been on the road for a while. Like us, they did not have a destination or a time frame in mind. I wondered if I sounded like them when travel questions came up. I did.

With the fear I would not fit into my riding gear anymore, we moved back to Marias Pass Summit, Polebridge at a lower elevation also getting a bit warm. One morning, I watched two campers packing up their motorcycles a few spaces away. They must have pulled in late as I had not heard any noise. I could see them through the trees surrounding us. One tent. I could tell and hear they were father and son. The son must have had polio as he limped while his knees stayed together, one child step at a time. I could not help but approach them and we started chatting about their journey. The son lived with his parents, indeed a father and son outing, quality time for both of them. A couple hundred miles every day, a few photos, cooking their breakfast and dinner and eating out for lunch. The son surprised me how well he handled his bike while they pulled away waving. Happy for them, my thought that morning "They are doing it".

We spent much time at the Glacier. The territory immense and present always, the couple hubs, East and West Glacier to mingle within, quite often bumping into souls such as us being present in the same fashion. The weather, always the main character, changed daily with its many personalities. I found out a tornado hit Madison County, not too far away, with winds up to 90 mph causing much damage. It hailed nonstop for three days giving me the bright idea to get a motel room in East Glacier. The least inexpensive rate? $140 a night. We came back to the summit that same afternoon and reset camp. Bad days, good days, we stayed out. The rough ones were the price to pay for the pleasant ones. When we emerged from the dark and somber days, the rays of sunshine literally lifted my heart. The soul would start smiling as the physical freedom reinstated while in shock, often asking myself "What do we do now? Which was normal? Today or yesterday?" Was there even such a thing as normal or is it the total array of the darkness and brightness in sequence just as life, being the complete package. Continuous sunny days would not allow us to appreciate them. Throw in a couple storms, a few wet days, and the value of the sunshine would surface stronger than ever wanting to savor its moments. Too much of a good thing loses its value quickly unless turned over and faced with the other side.

Spirit! Always amazing me. So totally in the moment taking it all in. Good and bad weather. Cooped up in the tent or laying on his bed inside Sherpa, riding in plain sunshine. Goggles and helmet on. *"He is your friend, your partner, your defender, your dog. You are his life, his love, his leader. He will be yours, faithful and true, to the last beat of his heart. You owe it to him to be worthy of such devotion. Always be who your dog thinks you are."* I don't know who had written this, but I liked it when I stumbled on those words. I think Spirit was ready to move on. Maybe myself as well, leaving the unseen for next time.

Big Horn National Forest intrigued my curiosity. Not too far and with a few weeks of summer left, we headed in that direction. Off and on we did well taking the back roads. Back to Browning, Highway 89 south to Choteau where we picked up Highway 287 south and with no choice a bit of Freeway 15. We headed east on Highway 12, arriving in Helena while passing Canyon Ferry Lake on our left. Somewhere along the way, I intentionally made a wrong turn going north instead of south. We ended up spending the night in the little town of White Sulfur Springs. A nice error. It did smell like sulfur and the old train wagons on the side of the road caught my nostalgic attention. Main Street was deserted with inviting signs, no takers other than in the couple bars where, when we walked by, I could hear the outbursts of maybe one too many beers. A town of 1,000 or so in the past, mining as usual being the main industry had closed down. The sheepherders and their dogs moved away, same with the new generation gone urban. We picked up Highway 89 south the next day through Ringling, named by one of the Circus brothers who moved there years ago. Wilsall came next. I recalled being there before and having one of the best cheeseburgers in the country. The restaurant was still closed being too early. I did not want to wait around. I remembered the Mercantile store across the street having some of the best cinnamon rolls. The smells were not present. They did not have any that morning. We moved on. It was not meant to be.

We arrived on busy Freeway 90. One where the speed picks up with the visible concentrated fumes floating and the fuel stations mere impersonal oasis of myriads of trucks and cars. Drivers trying to avoid fender benders while munching on a day old burrito killed again from a one minute zap in a microwave. Everyone mindless with a haggard look and a phone at their ear while gesticulating their latest news to whomever. No choice but to join the bandwagon all the way to Columbus where we would finally get off, back roads always so welcoming. Highway 421 took us to Highway 212 through Joliet, we zigzagged in all directions and eventually Highway 310 took us to Lovell, through Silesia, Fromberg, Bridger and Wade. Big Horn ahead of us and looking forward roaming through unknown territory. We stopped at the Ranger Station as we always do for insight information. Pleasant and knowledgeable lady at the front desk with her undivided attention. I listened about the lay of the land, the decent roads, the rugged ones, dispersed camping, weather prediction and a bit of history going back a few thousand years. She finished with much information on Bighorn Canyon. I really did not want to hear of any space at lower elevations and setting up in a campground. Not wanting to be rude, I took the pamphlet. Back on the road after double checking everything, mentally and physically prepared for some steep uphills and switchbacks, on we went until we passed Highway 37 on our left, the entrance to Bighorn Canyon. One glance and a mile later I made a U-turn.

Red rocks, magentas, shapes of ghosts left over from the past, patches of green shrubberies, mauves and browns and all in between glistening from the harsh afternoon sun. Desert! I so much longed for it. A new home. No more cloned trees and curtailed vision from the forests. I pulled out the in-depth all mapped out pamphlet, the one I did not want to look at. A canyon, a reservoir, a couple campgrounds. We pulled into the first one and found out they were free. We picked the best view. No campers between us and the shore, bathrooms not too far and we had a covered picnic table. Utah, Big Bend, the Wyoming Red Desert, all came back to mind lifting me up. The winds picked up as Spirit laid out tanning and myself reading, trying to, while everything from the ground up trembling and shaking. Such background manipulated the remaining reflections of my life, witnessing their dance as such settings themselves having grown and matured, building their daily strength. Just as we had. It became a furious welcome to the canyon, the skies darkening and menacing. We seemed to be the only ones standing and facing what could turn into a rampage. Deep grays everywhere mixed in with black clouds for good measure. All lasted until sunset when far upon the horizon a patch of blue allowed some light on the stage. No rain, lightning or thunder but a rehearsal for another day's more violent storm.

Up early the next morning, I stuck my head out realizing I had enough time for my coffee and a walk to the water. All before sunrise to witness the red rocks taking on their robe of the day while the sun slowly dressed them up. With no one around that early, I left Spirit behind since lost in his sleep and most likely in a good dream, one about chasing a rabbit. My wool hat kept me warm, my camera dangled at my side as I reached the shore quickly, wanting a front row seat. Then it happened. Slowly, yet too fast. The rocks started pulling up their nightgowns and from shade to light all became a gradual change of clothes. Behind me, the sun's rays were at first shyly glancing into the skies as to make sure everything was alright. Next to me, the water, once a greyish blue, imitated the rocks and took on their yellowish golden hue as to assure them of its own worth. All became surreal losing the feel of the ground I was standing on. Such a gift that morning.

Spirit was still asleep when I returned. What a bum, yet I let him live his own life. I woke him for his walk, his nose to the ground the smells must have been good that day as his tail never stopped wagging. Breakfast time. More coffee, scrambled eggs, Spirit's bowl filled with two cups of food and we ate together. Colorful and tasty, it set me up for the beautiful day ahead within this new found treasure. The thermostat could not have been set any better, with a nice breeze blowing the clouds came back early protecting us from any heat.

The days lingered into a familiar timeless zone. The blue morning skies daily would slowly make room by afternoon for the welcomed clouds. The late storms were hit and miss while watching their progress. The temperatures rose, so did the humidity, and at some point, I knew we would leave for the higher elevations of Bighorn National Forest. I learned of much history within the present challenging land of this canyon, all before the dam was built. The Bighorn River being too treacherous and steep walled to navigate on, the early residents were forced to devise unusual strategies of survival. The hunters drove herds of game into land traps and gathered wild roots and seeds to balance their meat diet. They made clothes of skins, baskets and sandals from plant fibers and their tools out of rocks, bones and wood. Many battles took place as the years passed. Eventually, mining and cattle ranching came into play. It was not until 1966 that the Canyon became a National landmark.

We looked forward going up the mountains. We first stopped in Lovell, backtracking a few miles. We needed more provisions, check my messages, e-mails, reconnect with the world making sure it was still spinning. I easily found the library. Many messages were waiting to be heard and read. A few of them from my Mother having not talked to her in a while. I called her right away. She sounded good and yet tired, at no time honestly telling me how she really felt, never wanting to worry me. It is a good time of the year in Munich she said and as my plans continuously in Jell-o, we both decided I would go visit her for a couple of weeks. She really wanted to see me. I could hear it in her voice. Bighorn National Forest would have to wait until the next time around. And what are friends for? A phone call to Colorado Springs, Shawn and Kathy would keep Spirit for my time away. With three dogs themselves, a nice fenced backyard, I had no doubt Spirit would daily give a nice run to his playmates. With good timing, we pulled into Colorado Springs 600 miles later.

All packed up after a nice dinner, the early flight seemed even longer this time around with a stopover in Atlanta. Nothing new besides the latest movies. The seats tighter than ever and the food just as bland. There was no sense getting upset at the long lines while approaching customs, the fast paced foot traffic when changing gates and no consolation with only fast food facing me in every hallway of the airports. The dark skies of Munich welcomed me and so did the brightly lit face of my Mother. She had of course aged a bit. A few more wrinkles, a bit slower, a bit harder of hearing. A taxi took us to her apartment where once again, displayed everywhere, photos of Lance, grandparents, distant family members, all stared at me. I even saw myself from years past with curly hair and a mustache. Another one of my aunt in her younger years while alone on stage giving a piano recital in front of thousands. As the days went on and more often than not, left alone while my Mother rested, I wondered what had happened. A silly question truly which encompassed many others. Those days in Munich became a mile marker. Throughout past times never quite realizing the calendar marching on, a big block of life had vanished and the photos were the only reminders of such past.

We went out for short jaunts during my visit. She tired quicker. Times were cozy in her apartment. Some days we did not even go anywhere, only cooked and talked a lot. The living room shelves and the see through cabinets showed empty spaces having given much away in case she would move. I really did not quite believe her and never, unlike in past times, brought up such a move to the United States. Not even for winter times, a few months which I always thought would be nice for her to get out of the cold, snow and ice. I did not think she could travel alone anymore and we came up with a scenario about me coming back and bringing her over. Just in case. She had mildly brought it up. My hopes had vanished by then and we just enjoyed the present moments.

Quite a story teller as I sat for hours listening and trying to comprehend our family genealogy of which I had only heard bits and pieces. She told it all this time. From as far back as she could remember or read. Great grandparents and their lineage, their escape from the wars, the births and the marriages while everyone moved from one country to another. She covered our own world history and at the end I remained the last of the Mohicans. Some day my last name will not exist anymore. There is no one left but me.

The two weeks flew by quickly and so torn up leaving her behind. Spirit waited, the road called, winter approaching fast and we needed to get to The Oasis. So much controversy within those days. So many unanswered questions. Such an apprehensive feeling as if I was defecting. Lost in my thoughts, Colorado Springs welcomed me and so did Spirit happier than ever and in great shape. As in the few earlier winters, The Oasis was ready for us with open arms. It felt as this time around the journey had been a long one. Both exhausted, we only slept and ate the first few days. I could not get passed my Mother's image all alone in her apartment. I knew how rough winters were in Munich and aware she did not heat every room as the cost of power was prohibitive. I felt it all being so wrong. We ended up talking on the phone every day, as she also did with her sister who lived in Belgium, while I planned to return as soon as possible. On the physical side, I managed to tear a right upper arm muscle and my back was starting to hurt. The doctor said it would take time to heal. That was one luxury I could afford, but as usual I became impatient, mornings being the worse and poor Spirit endured a bit more hibernation than in past winters. We had food, fuel, shelter and for myself, many books to read. To make matters worse the weather turned into incessant rains. The list of "things to do" needed to wait having to work on my patience. The pains slowly went away as did a few weeks. Not being at my my best, lucky me, Spirit never let me down, having been a closer shadow since my return never leaving my sight, watching my every step. An intense bond and his ability to listen so powerful.

The present faced me with a more than ever important need of regrouping. Binding together all those years past, going over the lessons learned, some I knew awaiting. Had I come to terms losing my only child and best friend? Not really. Here and there, not too often, but it did happen, a hate mail would still make its way on my screen. They did not move me as they used to, as by then I felt sorry for the messenger. They showed me the kind of world we lived in. I never wanted to believe there were bad people out there. After those e-mails, I emerged from my naivety and understood the simple painful fact of a few roaming the earth. Hitting below the belt, they must have been real unhappy people, while including my Mother among their insults. I never quite understood why they took the time to read our journal and find me. I called it "The balance of life". There are the poor and the rich, the healthy and the unhealthy, tall and short, peaks and valleys, you name it. Everything and everyone along with their opposite. Why not the good people and the bad ones as well. I often wondered why they were even called human beings.

I missed the concept of having family nearby. Some togetherness as in my childhood, when with grandparents, uncles, aunts, nieces and nephews, we would gather around many meals on weekends and festivities. I knew all of this was due to the fact my Mother being so far and our family scattered around the world. Coming up in her years, I felt I should be with her instead of so far away and thought about moving back to Europe for a while. It would have been a logistical nightmare to do so with Spirit and I could not afford the expenses. The Oasis welcomed us with open arms but also threw me in a state of confusion never experienced before. Lance's birthday was coming up, Christmas, the New Year, his anniversary. All these days were bundled up covering a span of those few months.

Sherpa became extremely helpful with a sore shoulder even if the notion of jumping in a car and going seeming odd never left me. Some days arrived where I took advantage of it when cold and feeling lazy. The car allowed us to stay out late in Terlingua while Spirit would be sheltered, as more musicians were showing up to play on the weekends. I found an outlet that occupied me which I enjoyed. Being around much music and making videos of those times. I called those months "the musical winter". The local musicians gathered on Terlingua Porch throughout many Sundays, sometimes up to a dozen, all playing together and a few passerbys dancing. Blues, Blue Grass, old and new Country Music and everything in between. These were good times and I felt fortunate the musicians did not mind a camera pointed at them. A new calling as I learned how to edit the videos. We started going to town a couple times a week as a few out of towners also started to beautifully perform. A world renown cello player, a beautiful mysterious and soothing voice from Austin playing her guitar, a classical quartet one evening, a new path found so enlightening. Even the American Legion a few miles away started having a monthly jam.

Indeed, a winter taking inventory of our life. Trying to look forward, yet my living in the present did not allow much of that vision. The now border-lined the past stronger than the future, especially when some dates came up. I realized the powerful and positive changes within as I started rereading my own journal and going through the 100,000 or more photos taken, by this time, seven years behind us. Our journal that winter saw the three million visitors mark and affected many more lives than ever imagined. It all came about from the one day when I decided writing would be our best therapy. We now had a home, something I never planned on either. It just happened, like everything else coming along our way. I wanted us to be at The Oasis, I also wanted us on the road towards those unknown destinations. Every time I looked at the weather and demographic map of the country, I realized how good The Oasis is. Again we stayed.

Whenever we stopped by the Porch in Terlingua for the first time when arriving, everyone present, meaning the daily locals, would stand up and shake my hand, now both considered locals. Always the same questions. "When did we return?" " How long are we staying?" " How nice to see you again" and mainly "How is Spirit doing"? Most, hardcore residents spending their summers in 120 degree heat. I respected that and often wished we could do the same. Sometimes. There could not have been any boredom being here. We still had not seen everything including the two parks. Going to towns was always one of many choices. Alpine or Marfa? Fort Davis or Marathon? Sometimes a few more rides to Presidio. A good place to be.

The skies turned eerie on the eve of Lance's birthday. Yet, there appeared a rainbow on the distant horizon left of Nine Points. Lightning turned the desert into daylight flashing the already soaked grounds and creating shadows of the creosotes. The air itself rumbled like two armies facing each other for a battle to the end. Sitting, drenched on a log by my Center of the Universe, I felt the earth itself shake from such madness. A moment arrived when silence prevailed. Just when I thought the fight would be over, one more canon replied toward its adversary. And another one, and a few more as by then the drops of rain turned into bullets and I became caught in the cross fire. There was no escape as I did not want to. Were we shouting? Talking? I would never know nor ever forget such a powerful night as I wrote *"What an incredible entrance to tomorrow this is. There was no need for such a reminder my loved one. I am with you every moment and day even when you might think I am not because I have learned to smile and laugh. That is what you would have me wanted me to be as such. Right? It is as if I make it through this admirable show of forces, I can make it through anything else. I have, we have through the past seven years. Up and down, any which way thrown at me, the constant flow of the letters of your sweet name has never left my soul. What is in store for us? Or do I really want to know?"*

I started taking better inventory of my friends. Trying to define friends and acquaintances. I started grading my friends. "A friends", "B friends" and so forth. I wanted to stop at "D friends", but since turning my back on the many commercial entities, there were now many "Z friends".

The truth was, those "Z friends" vanished into thin air. The characterizations and interpretations of our "A friends" had been created with time, as well as the amount of trust they projected and vice versa. Most of the rest of the alphabet rubbed me raw, the trust vanished. Sadly enough I came to the conclusion they only wanted to hang on to us because, supposedly, we were in their word, "famous". I never thought we were. I considered us a team having chosen a healthy life, which sometimes as with every compromise lined with a few rough cobblestones. We both wore "one face" and always proud of that fact. Not long ago others faces I stared at were only illusions and smoking mirrors. Much contents from our journal and photo galleries were being taken without permission or asking. I would have gladly given them away. As the expression in French calls it "fais accomplis", meaning "taking", and "then asking". I received an e-mail after writing about all this including the subject of watermarks on photos I felt compelled to use. Someone coming forward wrote he had indeed stolen a photo, which regardless protected or watermarked can be done. I wrote back telling him I appreciated his honesty and mentioned their price of only one dollar a download in their medium size. An extra dollar the next day arrived in my account with a thank you note. I read in his signature line he was a pastor. I smiled. It became the principle of it all including respect and honesty, such adjectives continuously lacking, a matter of priorities reshuffled for a better life.

A sense of freedom came upon me that winter, even if disappointed with myself for not seeing soon enough the ongoing destructive path rolling toward us. I tightened up and devoted my energy towards my few "A friends" remaining. They were gold to me and still remain the core of our lives. We are very fortunate. *"When we get out of the glass bottle of our ego and when we escape like the squirrels in the cage of our personalities and get into the forest again, we shall shiver with cold and fright. But things will happen to us that we don't know ourselves. Cool, inlaying life will rush in." [D.H. Lawrence]*

A winter of decompression, riding being the key as my shoulder healed. During moderate weather, when a full moon rose in the sky, we would go to sleep by late afternoon, then get up around midnight and ride until morning not needing headlights on the familiar dirt roads surrounding us. Magical rides to nowhere. Up and down the hills, crossing empty creek beds, right or left, it did not matter as we traveled through the black and white landscape lined with shadows of cactus creating sometimes imaginary characters of all sizes and shapes. Almost eerie at times when all notion of distances and dimensions changed. I imagined predators surrounding us and Spirit being my savior protecting me. No man's land as everyone was asleep. Not a single other vehicle or soul.

Few visitors ever stopped by The Oasis too far from Terlingua and its action taking place in the bars and restaurants. About 40 miles. The distance a big inconvenience, and maybe too much silence here. Silence for many can be scary and lonely. Loneliness can turn into fear. A couple from England did stop by for a few days while traveling to Belize with their four wheel drive Russian Lada car. Liz, Chris and their dog John, Spirit in doggie heaven having a companion to play with. They had been on the road for a while after crossing the ocean. In this day and age when the "Chrome Hummer" syndrome mostly prevails with mega-horse turbo engines advertised heavily for drooling affects, their little $3,000 Lada was a refreshing sight. No chrome hubcaps, air conditioner, glitter in the paint or 16 speakers. A basic four cylinder engine, four wheel drive, a winch, locking hubs and hand crank windows. What a concept! There was no need to explain about conserving water, solar power, the compost toilet or the harshness of the land. They previously by themselves floated the Amazon River for four months with only a folding canoe. No illusions were present during their wonderful visit. We did not talk about Holiday Inns or Five Star restaurants. They got a flat tire at one point and I helped them change their punctured 16" tube with a 15" one. Them out of spares, that is all I had. We shot a video of the experience and while watching it over a couple times, I saw myself in a different light. Filled with humor and laughter as never before. How strongly the forward momentum of those past years affected me! Words from a reader reached me *"Yes, life throws some right hooks in every now and then, but the total sum is of grandness, a greatness beyond speculation that life is the gift, that earth itself is the cathedral and wonder and joy and sometimes sorrows are the Holy Sacraments"*. *[Alaskan Rover]*

It was all right to be happy. As happy as I was going to be. The memories bright, they themselves filled with laughter and much love. It took a while to realize such aspects could be present and they did not have to only remain memories. As *Kahlil Gibran* wrote *"Your living is determined not so much by what life brings to you as by the attitude you bring to life. Not so much by what happens to you as by the way your mind looks at what happens"*.

The stage at The Oasis became of the utmost therapy along with my writing, which occurred almost daily. Every morning turned into a routine starting with a good cup of coffee, a short hike with Spirit, his breakfast, mine, and a few words on the journal. It seemed a long time since the day we left Georgia. It was only then that my apprehensions and confrontations faded away while surfacing for air as feeling asphyxiated for so long trying to find who I had really become. I knew the ladder had no end and its platform only a figment of my imagination. Constant growth, realizations, lessons, pages of awareness, the decision to make a right, a left, sometimes forward or backtrack. Clarity made room those days as a veil of lighter colors descended upon me, so beautiful the element of surprise would catch me off guard.

I avoided Art Walk in Alpine, the holidays spent with only Spirit. The need for peace and silence prevailed. Small talk those days did not move me feeling onto something bigger, a change taking place within after the many switchbacks we lived through. We both showed real smiles on our faces and felt so safe with each other in this vast desert surrounding us. Maybe some day I would be that old man with his long white hair and beard, his dog next to him. I would not menace the skies though. We continued going into the park where we camped a few days at a time. Always a nice change of scenery while avoiding the busy season. Alone, but not lonely, another step we climbed together, our backyard rarely shared. I thought at times of others stuck between their own cement walls. I wanted so much to convey the message to get out, to experience their own play area, one which remained free with no remote control and consisted of only one channel. The one which opened the minds, nurtured them, made one think and forget all at the same time which would make someone understand who they are by peeling away the many faces worn. There was nothing needed within Mother Nature but one's self. The rest had no values.

The days turned into that ocean with no ripples. I wanted to call it "perfection" as we reached new heights, my windows clearer and my vision sharpened. It made me think about the loss, or the gain, depending on how I looked at it, of past so-called friends vanishing. I so much wished for them to find the door knobs of their own spaces which were, unfortunately, only filled with their uncertain precarious and unsettled fame. To leave behind the book cover, that eye candy, and start instead reading into the depth of the chapters of life. I did miss them at times. They were not bad people, only a bit lost, hoping some day they would find a better path. As *Howard Zinn* said *"We were not born critical of existing society. There was a moment in our lives when certain facts appeared before us, startled us, and then caused us to question beliefs that were strongly fixed in our consciousness embedded there by years of family prejudice, unorthodox schooling, imbibing of newspapers, radio and television. This would seem to lead to a simple conclusion: that we all have an enormous responsibility to bring to the attention of others information they do not have, which has the potential of causing them to re-think long held ideas".*

We truly moved on while living on this endless road. We trekked around another circle traced as the past carrot, dangling bright and strong at one time while being an attraction as none before, had now wilted and rotted. That same circle which felt like a tight noose around my neck was no more as it grew limp and fell to the ground. Totally quitting the arena of magazine writing, rallies and everything else that followed gave us back the freedom we started with. The diplomas of life were covering our walls, leaving much space for more, yet the present ones mattered the most.

> *"You cannot escape Karma. It is what it is. It does not judge, it is neither good nor bad like most people think. It is the result of all the actions, positive and negative, a constant balancing act of events cause and effect, tit for tat reaping and sowing what goes around comes around. However you phrase it, it is the same in the end"* [Alyson Noel]

It was April of the same year, 2013, when my mother and I, on Easter day, spent a couple hours on Skype. On Monday, the day after, dark clouds moved in bringing with them lightning, thunder and much rain. That is the same morning the phone rang. The ring tone was not the same as a decade ago, the content was. I broke down becoming as dark as the skies of the moments above me. It was my uncle from Belgium calling me with the worst news ever. My Mother had suffered a massive stroke. Her neighbor found her on the door steps. She was in the hospital on life support.

My Mother passed away on April 12th at 7:30 a.m. in Munich where I had flown right away. Today, once again, we sit at The Oasis as 2014 rolled in. It has been ten months. She is buried on the east side of my Center of the Universe, joining Lance who is facing west. It has been a quiet winter, only going to town when needing food, drinking water, fuel or propane. I sit with them every day. We talk, we cry, we have started to smile again. The lessons from years past have resurfaced, yet, they are not filling the hole she left in my life. From the first time on that month of April when I flew to Munich, as I had to return one more time, I knew losing her would be hard. I never thought it was going to be this hard. We had been together after all for 65 years. It has taken a few months to write this book while my writing on our journal slowed down. Now that our past seven years are here within these pages, once again my daily thoughts are resurfacing in our journal. I did though write this a few days ago

"Regaining momentum lost as the gears are slowly turning again within these patches of silence so welcomed. The passion and the need for the road is resurfacing. The colors surrounding me, the sights, the smells and the shapes are again making their way into my consciousness. I have had good Human help from a friend with whom we reconnected after some silence. A true friend ready and willing to listen, one that felt a while back from miles away I needed the touch we all need throughout such times. A friend offering nurturing and wise words helping me rebuild my bridge crumbled just a few months ago. I feel lucky and fortunate as sometimes the loneliness after losing a Mother, a best friend, crumbles the path one has been on. Rare are such friends with their ears open to the true sounds of hardship willing to be on the giving end with an array of much needed support. The world has changed and the intensity of advancements in our technology, especially communication, has only pushed us backwards, inducing us with volume of social media and setting back the true human touch which once was present over a cup of coffee or an afternoon spent visiting. Quantity over quality has come to the forefront mixed in with superficiality scaring too many from divulging who they really are, what we really feel. Present is, wrongly so, the fear of *the fear recognizing our true human self which is still so in-depth beautiful and delicate".*

Our core, our wealth, our human monetary currency truly never changed. It is our heart, our love for each other that has always prevailed as it should. Those values often are down replaced by too many sparks of physical possessions, which in turn keeps everyone busy with the overtime needed to comply and locks the doors to our most valuable insights. Feel and truly support each other. Please.

"There is a sacredness in tears. They are not the mark of weakness, but of power. They speak more eloquently than ten thousand tongues. They are messengers of overwhelming grief and unspeakable love". [Washington Irving]

CPSIA information can be obtained at www.ICGtesting.com
Printed in the USA
BVOW02s1435150615

404658BV00004B/126/P